The Blueprints of Heaven

Seeing Heaven Revealed on Earth

TREVOR BAKER

RIVER

PUBLISHING

River Publishing & Media Ltd
Barham Court
Teston
Maidstone
Kent
ME18 5BZ
United Kingdom

info@river-publishing.co.uk

ISBN 978-1-908393-12-8

Printed in the United Kingdom

Contents

What Others Are Saying About This Book   4

Dedication   10

Foreword   11

Introduction   13

1. Convergence of Heaven and Earth   17

2. The Resources of Heaven   27

3. Your Restored Inheritance   33

4. Is the Church ready?   53

5. An Open Door Lifestyle   61

6. Angelic Visitations   73

7. Mantles of Anointing   85

8. Mantles and Relationships   95

9. The Kingdom of Heaven   107

10. Keys of the Kingdom   115

Endnotes   125

About the Author   128

What Others Are Saying About The Blueprints of Heaven

"Trevor Baker is a man who lives and operates in the power of the supernatural. His newest book, *The Blueprints of Heaven* is what God has for His sons and daughters who are truly hungry and thirsty to operate in the fullness of His Kingdom. It is filled with truths and revelations to arm and equip you with knowledge and understanding that will position you to enter into your rightful inheritance as co-heirs with the King of Glory."

Ché Ahn, Senior Pastor, HROCK Church

"Without God's power and salvation, mankind has no hope at all. I endorse Trevor's encouragement of every believer to take hold of the powers of the age to come through faith in Jesus, so that His Kingdom will be manifested as normal, everyday Christian life in this world. The only way to honor God is to accomplish His will on earth by His power. This book will increase the faith of everyone eager to live constantly in the Spirit, ready and able to do the works of Jesus!"

Rolland Baker, Co-Founder and Director, Iris Ministries

"Trevor Baker's new book is a dynamic read that gives every believer a road map into maturity in this hour. This book brings an in-depth revelation and teaching for this age of Christianity on how to operate as a kingdom-builder as well as being a corporate Church that knows how to bring the reality of Jesus on earth as He is in heaven. Trevor has done an amazing job at inspiring us to move beyond the 'milk' and into the 'meat' of a fully developed

God-journey that will take you from passion to release and possibly bring you across your tipping point into the greatness of your calling. It is that good!"

Shawn Bolz, Senior Pastor of Expression58

"With many years of experience and flowing in different streams Trevor has been one who has been pioneering the fresh dimensions of the Spirit and digging the wells that God has released in these days. His heart for God, his passion for the Spirit, his love for people and his desire for revival are all reflected in this book, alongside practical help to avoid the pitfalls on the way.

Derek Brown, Leader of KC21

"Trevor Baker is a practitioner not a mere theorist. Trevor intertwines his own personal testimony with teaching of experiencing a miracle-working, supernatural God. You may be stretched by the theology, but you will be encouraged by the testimony. I enjoyed this book and I'm sure you will too."

David Campbell, Regional Leader, Elim

"I am very excited to recommend Trevor Baker's book. Your life will be greatly enriched by the deep truths he reveals. Trevor and his wife, Sharon, are wonderful tools in the hand of God and the Spirit of God moves wonderfully in their lives. I give my full endorsement to this outstanding book."

Bobby Conner, Founder, Eagle's View Ministries

"One thing that is vitally needed in the 21st century Church is a thorough understanding of God's heart, plans and strategies to win this last day generation for His Kingdom. Trevor Baker, in his new book, goes right to the very heart of that issue and provides great insight with understanding into this all-important subject. In the decade that I have known Trevor, he has consistently exhibited not only a heart for the Lord and His Kingdom, but also a desire to see others functioning fully in their prophetic destiny and high calling. The book that you now hold in your hand is an expression of that desire and an invitation into the supernatural realm described by the early apostles and offered to the last day Church. In this book you will find understanding of spiritual doors, mantles of revelation and power, divine resources and the appropriation of our inheritance purchased by the Lord through His blood. All are vitally necessary ingredients for this last day Church."

Paul Keith Davis, Founder, WhiteDove Ministries

"*The Blueprints of Heaven* by my friend Trevor Baker will whet your appetite for more of Jesus and an even greater move of the Holy Spirit input generation. There needs to be a warning label on this book: When read, believed and acted on, the contents of this book will radically change your life!"

James W Goll, President, Encounters Network, Director, Prayer Storm

"Trevor Baker is a faithful man of God who has, over many years, by his and his wife Sharon's commitment and sacrifice to this ministry, proven his credentials to write a book such as this. I fully recommend Trevor's life and walk with God as an example amongst us today. Few have the grace of our heavenly Father on them as Trevor and his wife Sharon have and the power of the supernatural upon their lives and ministry is truly wonderful and an inspiration to us all. You will grow under Trevor's ministry through reading this book."

James Jordan, Director, Fatherheart Ministries

"Trevor Baker is a remarkable man - one who has the tenacity, energy and passion to press into the realm of the supernatural to embrace all that God has for us now. He asks halfway though this book, "Is the Church ready?" This book should provoke us all in our desire to press into God to uncover more of the reality of the Kingdom now."

Stewart Keiller, Leader, Bath City Church

"*The Blueprints of Heaven* is long overdue. Too many believers have lived in the misconception that they must wait until they get to heaven to access and utilize all its resources. The apostle Paul chided the Corinthians because they were, 'behaving like mere men.' Trevor Baker skillfully unfolds the truths of Scripture that help us to understand that we 'bear the image of the heavenly Man', and shows us how to draw from our heavenly inheritance now. Get ready – your life here on earth is about to take on a new dimension!"

Bill Prankard, Senior Pastor, Dominion Outreach Centre

"I have long believed that for God's Kingdom and His will to be done upon the earth as it is in heaven, someone has to see into the heavenly realms first. Trevor Baker lives a lifestyle of experiencing the supernatural heavenly realms of God. He has great fruit of these occurrences releasing heaven's resources. This book is scriptural and full of personal spiritual encounters that have the ability to bring you into supernatural activity on a regular basis. Your relationship with God the Father will be enhanced as you are empowered with Kingdom Keys. You will participate with the angelic and heaven's revelation to fulfill God's purposes as you read this book."

Dr. Sharon Stone, Senior Minister, Christian International Europe

"I have known Trevor Baker for perhaps 20 years. He is the real deal. Over these years he has grown in a prophetic healing anointing. This has been his passion and God has honored it and allowed him to see hundreds and thousands of healings and salvations. In his book Trevor describes how the intuitive and visionary abilities were present in his childhood and then, after salvation, were developed and grown into powerful spiritual faculties which God used to release His purposes on earth. It is inspiring reading as Trevor shares many amazing stories of supernatural encounters. It will raise your faith and give you a vision of what is possible for us to achieve in our Christian walk. It will release an impartation of faith into your heart."

Mark Virkler Ph.D. President, Christian Leadership University

"Many Christ-followers today are suffering from what I call the 'ache of the ordinary'. However, there is nothing ordinary about God. He is the Creator of all things and the most fascinating, awe-inspiring Being in all of creation ... He is GOD! So, why is it that so many Christians today seem to be so un-inspired in their relationship with Him? The answer is simply because many believers have simply not been awakened to the awesomeness of our God, nor have they been taught how to have real relationship with Him, beyond an initial salvation prayer. I highly recommend this book by my good friend, Trevor Baker, because I believe within it are many keys to intimacy with God that will answer the longing within every believer. Devour this book and decide to no longer live with the 'ache of the ordinary', but rather to live every day of your life filled with fascination and awe in the one who created you!"

Ryan Wyatt, Founding Lead Pastor, Abiding Glory Church

Dedication

To Sharon my wife and friend. Thank you for walking this journey into the heavenly realms with me. You have encouraged, trusted and believed in me to go further in my pursuit of God. You are a shining example of a woman of noble character.
You have given me so much.

Nicky & Paul.
You are in a Cross over season
when what you have pursued is
now to come into fulness.
     Go in and possess. all.
       Blessings
       Trevor.

Ex 33 v 14
Gal. 1 v 12.

Foreword

The Blueprints of Heaven is the story of a journey. The author, Trevor Baker, was a sensitive young man who God began to speak to. And the supernatural lifestyle that started at his conversion has continued throughout his walk with the Lord. He has only moved forward, following the progressive moves of God.

One of the great things to be said of anyone is that they navigated well the changing seasons of the Holy Spirit. Trevor has done just that. His hunger for more of God has kept him pliable and always in the middle of whatever God is doing. He's hungry, and God trusts him.

If this book were only his testimony, it would be worth it. But it's so much more. In it you will find great encouragement, wonderful insights, and brilliant testimonies of how God speaks to and works through this man. It is sure to draw the reader into the same quest that Trevor has been on for his entire life in Christ: the quest for the heart of God. To read the pages of this book is to read the hunger written on the heart of a man passionate for more, and equally passionate to impart and equip.

Bill Johnson
Bethel Church, Redding, CA
Author, *When Heaven Invades Earth* and *Face to Face with God*

Introduction

I believe that one of the attacks of the enemy has been to blind the eyes of believers to the realities of the supernatural realm, where we see God's dwelling place and experience supernatural activity on a regular basis. When John, the disciple whom Jesus loved, was imprisoned on the island of Patmos he received the following invitation:

"After this I looked, and there before me was a door standing open in heaven. And the voice I had first heard speaking to me like a trumpet said 'Come up here.'" (Revelation 4:1)

I believe this same invitation is given to every disciple loved by Jesus – the whole Church. One of my main purposes in writing this book is to encourage and help people to respond to that call. My desire is that you also will be able to, "Come up here" and experience heavenly realms.

Although the call to John is recorded in the last book in the Bible, I believe it speaks of the restoration of God's original purposes for mankind and has to be set within the context of those purposes. So in part 1 of this book, I begin by outlining God's purposes and man's inheritance: God dwelling with a people who reign on earth on His behalf. I discuss what God has done to make possible the restoration of man's inheritance and how we can best co-operate in that restoration process.

I also discuss, with reference to Scripture and to my own experience, various aspects of the supernatural realm, including the anointing of the Holy Spirit, mantles, and the ministry of angels. This is to demonstrate how much God is willing to make heaven's resources available to us so that we can help to fulfil His purposes to bring His Kingdom, His reign, on earth.

I can see this process in operation as I look back over my own life and ministry. I have seen God do immeasurably more than I could ask or imagine. Thousands of people have been healed, delivered and rescued from the dominion of darkness and brought into the Kingdom of the Son of God. I have also experienced the "immeasurably more" joy of lingering in His presence. But even as I rejoice in these things, I know that the restoration of God's purposes, of man's inheritance, is far from complete. There is always more.

It has always amazed me that the disciples, seeing what Jesus did and said, did not ask Him how to minister healing more successfully, be better at driving out demons, or to more effectively communicate with people. The only thing they ever asked Jesus to teach them was how to pray.

When Jesus taught His disciples to pray, He said,

"This then is how you should pray: 'Our Father in heaven.'" (Matthew 6:9)

His first revelation or unveiling regarding the practice of prayer is that it is built on relationship. Jesus probably used the Aramaic word Abba, which Jewish children used when addressing their earthly fathers. But our relationship with even the best of human fathers is not what Jesus is pointing us to. The Father we seek a relationship with is found in heaven. This is quite a stretch for some people. In the natural, if we want to be with our father we have to go to the country, town and house where he lives. This is also true in the Spirit – we must go to our Father's dwelling place – heaven; and as Christians we can!

Do you ever wonder why the Church is not seeing the breakthrough that we desire to see on the earth? Jesus said in Matthew 6:10, "Your Kingdom come, Your will be done, on earth as it is in heaven." How is it that we do not see more miracles, signs and wonders? Is it because we do not really see what the Kingdom of heaven is like? How can we ask for the Kingdom of heaven to come if we have never seen it?! Of course, we receive some wonderful insights when we read God's Word, but what is heaven like today, in detail? What is happening there that we need to bring to earth?

Some of us need to have our perceptions radically changed, to become different people, people of heaven. We are often discouraged from deepening our spirituality by being told that we can become so heavenly-minded as to be of no earthly good. But we need to recognise the mindset underlying such statements which can be used as a device of the devil to lessen our desire to meet with our heavenly Father. Such a perspective allows us to foster unbelief until we no longer have faith to move in the unseen realm of the Spirit.

If you are tempted to listen to the voice of unbelief, remember that when Jesus taught His disciples it was not from an instruction manual. His teaching was born out of His own experience – the experience of a man who spent time in His Father's house, in heaven, and in heavenly realms.

So as you read, I pray that you will hear the Father say, as He said to Jesus, "You are my [child], whom I love; with You I am well pleased." (Luke 3:22). Then I hope that you will be encouraged to respond, with the apostle Paul in Philippians 3:14, "I press on toward the goal to win the prize for which God has called me heavenwards in Christ Jesus."

Chapter 1
The Convergence of Heaven and Earth

I believe that hidden in the heart of every person there is a desire to engage with another world – a realm that exists outside of their day-to-day earthly experience. Those with a limited knowledge of God and His ways, grasping for a deeper spiritual experience, have sought an "out of body" or "mind" experience. Those who have sensed the existence of a spiritual realm, but who lack the vocabulary to describe it have talked about possessing a "sixth sense". Whatever language people may use to describe it, each human being possesses an innate desire to experience life in a different dimension.

Many people have early childhood experiences related to this desire – often manifest in the form of dreams of being able to fly or to breathe whilst swimming under water. Such dreams echo our desire to explore another world as if it was real. All of us, at some point, want to visit Narnia or some other world where children become princes and princesses, where we live as heroes and fight battles, overcome enemies and live out adventures.

As a young boy I loved to watch a TV programme called "The Invisible Man". The central character, when dressed in certain clothes, was able to make himself invisible. Whenever he did so, he was able to go places and see things that other people couldn't. It was precisely this ability he had – to move in an unseen realm – that made the programme so enjoyable for me. I used to imagine what it would be like to observe events and yet remain unseen. Extending that thought, I used to spend time wondering what it would be like to be able to see things even before they happened and to be able to tell others about what would happen prior to the event taking place. Looking back, it was as though God had begun to awaken in me the dream of experiencing the supernatural that had He planted in me from conception.

Throughout my youth I would "daydream", and in these dreams I would imagine events that might take place. Sometimes this imagining of events would begin to encroach on reality. I can remember very vividly one such occasion. I was fifteen years old at the time and one day, as I was cycling home from school, the following thought struck me: "The propeller shaft of the QE2 has buckled on her sea trials and she is being towed back to Southampton." The date was November 13, 1968. When I arrived home I relayed this piece of "information" to my Mum. She looked at me quizzically and asked, "What are you talking about?" She commented that the ship had only just been built and had read in the news that it was only just beginning its sea trials. In response I simply said, "Well, watch the news and see for yourself what has happened." I was so sure that what I had seen in my mind had actually taken place that I was convinced the evening news would bear it out. So at six o'clock we watched the news and the headlines said, "The QE2 is being towed back to Southampton due to engine failure." I remember my mum saying to me, "Are you psychic or something? How did you know? Had you heard the news already?" Suddenly feeling vulnerable and embarrassed I told her that I had seen the news on my way home from school, but of course, I hadn't.

I believe that many people have these types of supernatural experiences, but which go unnoticed for most of their lives. They pay little or no attention to the thoughts they have, and never speak them out, so they remain just thoughts. They are brushed off as "intuition" and not recognised as echoes of the spiritual realm.

In my youth, there were many occasions when there was a knock at our door and I could clearly tell who was going to be standing there before the door was opened. I could "predict" it so accurately that it became a game I would play with my brother and sister. Other people can testify to similar experiences. These and other encounters can make us more open to the spiritual realm. Once this door is opened in our lives, however, it can become very easy to be susceptible to either godly or ungodly influences – especially when we are going through difficult times in our lives. At such times, if we are open to them, spiritual forces can seek to draw us into a dark realm.

When I was seventeen I had kind of vision of what the end of the world might look like. I arrived home late that night and talked with my Mum and Dad about it. During the early hours of the following morning I was awoken by my father who was in a state of panic and shock. He came to my sister and me explaining anxiously that something terrible had happened to my mother. I went with him into their bedroom and we thought that my mother was lying unconscious. In fact, she had died. I tried to resuscitate her, but to no avail. The trauma and shock of this experience and my failed attempt to bring my mother back to life left me with a recurring question: is death really the end of life or is there another realm that we are able to pass into where my mother had now gone? And could we enter this realm during this life as well as through death?

These were not normal thoughts for a seventeen-year old and I quickly realised that neither my family nor friends had the answers I so desperately sought to the questions I had. During the weeks that followed I imagined my mother being present in some way and wanted to make contact with her. I was convinced that the physical realm around me was not all that there was to the world and I pondered over and over if there was any way in which I could release my mind to embrace the world "beyond" – the world where people went when they died. Unfortunately, I attempted to do this through the use of drugs. I began experimenting with all kinds of substances, especially so-called "mind expanding" drugs.

I had used both drugs and alcohol recreationally in the past to have a good time, but now I was using them to relieve the pain of losing my mother, to numb the overwhelming grief which overtook me. I also found that I was now able to induce an altered state of being through drugs. This marked a major turning point in my life and I was plunged into a very dark world. During this time I was introduced to a spiritualist who had experienced a form of spiritual transport. He would leave his body and go to people, bringing healing by removing diseased organs from their body. I shared a house with him and he would spend time relating these experiences, offering to impart this ability to me.

Although I carried a deep longing to know and experience this spiritual realm, I somehow knew that if I experienced what this man was offering it would lead me into an even darker place than I had already known – and something or "someone" was drawing me away from that path. I knew I had to move out of this person's home.

At the same time I was getting more involved in drugs. I was twenty-one years old, addicted to drugs and still with no real answers to my searching questions. I registered at an addiction clinic; I knew something had to change. I could not go on living this life where I was so desperate for some spiritual encounter that I could not access.

Things came to a head when on 13th July, the day before my twenty-first birthday, I was charged and sentenced to six months in prison for possession of drugs and allowing my premises to be used for taking drugs. Finding myself incarcerated, separated from family and friends, and withdrawing from drugs, I began to cry out for help. I had begun reading a New Testament which I'd been given in prison, so I began calling on God to help me. I soon noticed that every time I prayed, a Presence would enter my cell and I would be overwhelmed with a sense of peace.

I had appealed against my sentence and I was waiting to go to Crown Court in order for my case to be heard. It was while I was in the holding cells that somebody gave me a brochure which had a testimony of a young man who had been addicted to drugs and Jesus Christ had set him free. I remember praying and asking God to do the same for me. I told God that if I got my prison sentence overturned then I would go to the same place this young man had gone to – a Christian-run drug rehabilitation centre in the Cotswolds called "Life for the World".

When the day of my appeal came, I stood before the judge and awaited his verdict. He told me that the sentence was just, but nevertheless he was going to commute my sentence to run concurrently instead of consecutively. This had the effect of turning my two three-month sentences into one three-month sentence and meant I would be released within days. I am still amazed today at the power that a person's words can have upon someone else's life.

Two weeks later I was admitted to this Christian rehabilitation centre, on 2nd October, 1973. I remember going to a meeting that evening with all the young men who were at the centre. This was the first Christian meeting I'd ever been in and it seemed so real, like the people truly believed what they were saying and sharing. Together they began to sing the words of the song:

"Breathe on me breath of God, fill me with life anew, so I may love what thou doest love and do what thou would do. Breathe on me breath of God, so shall I never die, but live with Thee the perfect life for all eternity. Breathe on me breath of God, till I am only thine, till all this earthly part of me glows with thy fire divine."

As I sang this song along with them, I realised for the first time that this "breath" had not been imparted to me, so two days later on October 4th at 6:30am I went to see the Director of the centre and asked how that could happen for me. He then told me what Jesus Christ had done on the cross. I finally had an answer to all my searching: all of my former life had been forgiven and I could enter into a new life. I could know God and my spirit would be made alive. He then led me through a prayer and I received Jesus Christ as my Saviour and the One who could give me life, a real, spiritual life.

In the days that followed I sensed that at long last I had entered into a new realm – the invisible spiritual realm. This time, however, I didn't have to be afraid or run away from it; I could embrace it and allow the Holy Spirit to embrace me. I was beginning to see the world in a way I had never seen it before. Everything looked so clear and the colours looked so radiant.

It was during one of these days that I happened to be out walking in the countryside near the rehabilitation centre. It was a glorious autumn day and a golden sunset was enveloping the early evening sky. I had an overwhelming sense that finally I had been filled full of life and had found my place in this world that God had created. The more I thought about this, the more overwhelmed I seemed to become. I felt as though my heart was expanding within me. I could sense the presence of God so tangibly; it felt as though someone was following me. I turned half expecting to see someone, but instead I saw a wonderful amber and golden ball of light hovering on the opposite side of the woods where the sun was setting. It's hard to describe, but this wasn't sun, but a physical manifestation of God's glory and His presence. I was overwhelmed with fear, but not a terror-filled fear, an astounding fear – sheer awe. I was encountering another world, a world I had been created for and which had lain dormant, longing for me to wake up and experience it. There was a life God had prepared for me that wouldn't end with death. There were answers to the questions I'd had ever since my mother died.

Now as I turned, the glorious ball of light, shining with all its beauty, began to speak to me. The words seemed to echo and reverberate through my whole being. It was like something had "opened up" within me and as it opened a light shone in and I was given a vision that seemed to impose itself on my spirit, telling me what God was calling me to do. The only way I can explain this is to say that it was like a camera: as a picture is taken the shutter opens and light enters; what the lens is focused on becomes imposed upon the film. This is what happened in me – my spirit had been opened by God and His purpose for me imprinted on it.

After this amazing experience I rushed back to the centre, eager to tell the centre Director what had happened. Sadly, he told me that this vivid encounter was demonic in origin and that I should never seek this kind of experience again. These words had such an impact on me. I was both devastated and confused, but assumed that this man, an experienced Christian, must know more than me. The awareness of the spiritual realm that had been awakened in me was shut down – and it would remain closed for many years to come.

I am aware that for many people this has also been their experience. Too many have remained ignorant of the dynamic power available to them because they have not understood how to access the spiritual realm. Perhaps they have shared spiritual insights with those in authority, only to have them squashed. Often those in leadership, due to their own lack of understanding and inability to access spiritual power, have either deliberately or inadvertently shut down others, labelling their experiences "demonic". In so doing they have closed the door to the supernatural power of God and prevented His light from pouring into the darkness. Once this happens, vision and revelation begin to fade as the spiritual "shutters" remain closed.

I believe, however, that these are days when God wants to restore our awareness of the spiritual dimension. He is giving us back our spiritual eyes to see into the realm of the Spirit and witness what God is doing. Just as Jesus prayed, "Your will be done on Earth as it is in Heaven," we too are beginning to see the reality of heaven manifest on earth, so that we can be conduits through which God's glory is displayed on the earth.

I can remember so clearly the day when, after twenty years had passed with this realm being closed to me, God suddenly revealed Himself to me and restored all I had lost. By this time I was a minister and I was waiting on God to hear what I should share at our Friday evening renewal meeting where I would be speaking . As I lay in God's presence, I became aware of a small blue light. It was like the flash of an arc welding light, and yet it was constant. I leaned towards the light and as I did so it got bigger until it enveloped me. Then I heard these words: "The seal is broken. Now tell them the things that you have seen." This experience lasted for about twenty seconds. It was as though the spiritual shutter had been opened again and revelation flowed in. It was as if heaven had been opened up to me and the presence of Jesus became so real.

I remember going into the meeting and saying to my wife, Sharon, that we should be prepared for heaven to enter our meeting that night and as we began to worship there was a wonderful sense of His glorious presence breaking into our lives afresh. After a full three hours of worship, I spoke about the experience that I'd had before the meeting and as I did so, heaven descended; there was a convergence of heaven and earth. People throughout the meeting were taken into waking visions and began to prophesy, sharing the things that they were now seeing. A door had been opened into heaven and we were being invited into these heavenly places to experience the fullness of the spiritual blessings which had been stored up for us.

This book is the culmination of the years of seeking to continue to walk in the realm of the Spirit that followed. I invite you to embark on a journey to receive the blueprints of heaven and see heaven established on earth. This is what Jesus opened up when He walked on the earth and taught us to pray into being.

Chapter 2
The Resources
of Heaven

God's purpose in Creation

Isaiah 45:18 tells us that when God created the heavens and the earth, He formed the earth to be inhabited. "At one time the earth was formless and empty, and darkness was over the surface of the deep," Genesis 1:2 informs us. It seems that something cataclysmic had happened. This was, perhaps, the time of Satan's rebellion in heaven. But God fulfilled His purpose, speaking light into existence and then filling the earth with good things. The culmination of God's creation was man, made in God's image and charged with ruling the earth on His behalf.

God planted a pleasant garden in the east and "took the man and put him in the garden of Eden to work it and take care of it" (Genesis 2:15). But this garden was not simply where man was to live and work – it was also where God walked, a place where He could have fellowship and communion with Adam and Eve, communicating His heart to them and telling them more about His plans for His creation. It was a place where the rule and reign of heaven would be extended as Adam received and implemented God's will.

To enjoy fellowship with a people who would rule the earth in accordance with His wishes had always been God's desire and still is today. But man sinned by eating from the fruit of the tree of the knowledge of good and evil. God had already decreed that this act of disobedience would lead to death. Now God's justice demanded that Adam be banished from the garden and denied access to the tree of life. No longer would Adam live in the place where heaven and earth converged. God continued to show His concern for Adam and Eve, sacrificing an animal to make garments of skin for them, but man had lost the supreme privilege of fellowship with his Creator.

Bethel, the house of God

You can read about the convergence of heaven and earth in Genesis Chapter 28. In a dream Jacob sees a stairway resting on the earth with its top reaching to heaven and angels ascending and descending on it. Above the stairway he sees the Lord, who promises to bless him and his descendants.

Jacob's spiritual experience stays with him after he awakes. "Surely the Lord is in this place, and I was not aware of it," he says (Genesis 28:16). Jacob had witnessed how heaven is waiting to burst upon the earth, allowing God's power to be manifest in the lives of ordinary men and women. This experience of the convergence of heaven and earth is very powerful and, rightly so, Jacob was terrified by it. "How awesome is this place!" he said. "This is none other than the house of God; this is the gate of heaven" (Genesis 28:17). From that time on, Luz, the city where heaven and earth converged for a time, became known as Bethel, meaning "the House of God".

The tabernacle and the temple

Later God gave instructions for the building of a tabernacle, and subsequently a temple, where He could live among men, His presence manifest on the earth. When Moses had completed the tabernacle it became a place of habitation for His presence:

"...the cloud covered the Tent of Meeting, and the glory of the Lord filled the tabernacle. Moses could not enter the Tent of Meeting because the cloud had settled upon it, and the glory of the Lord filled the tabernacle." (Exodus 40:34-5)

Later, when Solomon completed the temple, we read in 1 Kings 8:10-11 how heaven invaded earth once again:

"When the priests withdrew from the Holy Place, the cloud filled the temple of the Lord. And the priests could not perform their service because of the cloud, for the glory of the Lord filled his temple."

So God once again had a geographical dwelling place among mankind. But man's access to this special place of His presence was incredibly restricted. The place of meeting was above the mercy seat, the cover of the ark of the covenant, which was placed in the Most Holy Place (the Holy of Holies), the inner sanctuary of the tabernacle and temple. The only time recorded in Scripture that man went into the Most Holy Place was when the high priest entered on the Day of Atonement, when sacrifices were made to atone for the nation's sins. So just once per year a single human experienced the manifest presence of God.

A single geographical place of meeting is very vulnerable. The Lord became so angry with Israel's continued sin that He eventually withdrew from the temple and, lacking God's protection, Israel was soon conquered and the temple destroyed. Although the temple was subsequently rebuilt by the returning exiles, there is no record of it becoming God's dwelling place again.

So we understand that in the generations between the Fall of Adam and the Birth of Jesus, God dwelt with man for a limited time only and under restricted circumstances. We could express this by saying that heaven was open only partially and intermittently. But this was all to change with the coming of Jesus.

Jesus' birth and baptism

Jesus' birth was announced by angelic beings, messengers from heaven and the realm of heaven burst upon the earth once again. Years later, at His baptism, heaven was opened again.

"As He was praying, heaven was opened and the Holy Spirit descended on Him in bodily form like a dove. And a voice came from heaven: 'You are my Son whom I love; with You I am well pleased.'" (Luke 3:21-2)

Through Jesus' presence on the earth and His infilling with the Holy Spirit the house of God no longer resided in a city. It was no longer tied to a structure, a building or a geographical location, such as Bethel – it now resided in a person, Jesus. God no longer dwelt in a man-made tabernacle or temple, but in the temple of Jesus' body. Jesus foresaw a renewing of the angelic activity revealed to Jacob. He promised Nathanael, "You shall see heaven open, and the angels of God ascending and descending on the Son of Man." (John 1:51)

Jesus went about expressing the power of God's kingdom as, by the power of the Spirit, He "saw" into heaven and enacted God's will on the earth. He modelled an entirely new way of God's presence being manifest on the earth. Jesus ushered in a new season in which man would again be able to bring to earth God's Kingdom, God's rule and God's will. Matthew 4:17 and 24 express this well: "From that time on Jesus began to preach: 'Repent, for the Kingdom of heaven is near'" or as I prefer to say, it is within our reach! And, "Jesus went throughout Galilee teaching in their synagogues, preaching the good news of the Kingdom, and healing every disease and sickness among the people."

God does not want anyone to perish and through Jesus' sacrifice and death on the cross, our sins can be forgiven and our fallen state restored. The first Adam was banished from God's presence. Now, through the work of the last Adam, Jesus, we are welcomed into the presence of our loving, merciful Father. Then, as He extends His love to us, we in turn love Him (1 Corinthians 15:45).

After Jesus returned to His Father, the Church became the dwelling place, the household of God. Paul reminds us that we, as individuals and corporately together, are the temple of the Holy Spirit. 2 Peter says that we are like living stones, being built into a spiritual house.

Heaven was opened with the coming of Jesus. It remains open and will never be closed. This is a key truth for us to grasp and understand. The Church can and must enter into the inheritance planned by God before the foundation of the world. We can walk with God in unhindered fellowship in the cool of the day, and we can call on the resources of heaven in helping to bring God's Kingdom on earth. Each of us needs to rise up and embrace this reality.

Chapter 3
Your Restored Inheritance

How do you see things?

There is a phrase that says, "Perspective is everything". I'm sure many will have seen the "optical illusion" image that either looks like a vase or the outline of two faces looking at each other. Which you see is determined by your perspective.

There are times when the Church's perspective – it's core view of itself – is very different from God's perspective. Often we can be so wrapped up in ourselves and busy with our lives that we gradually drift from God's will for us. This is not a new problem. We see recorded in the book of Revelation, Jesus' views on a number of churches. Look at His comments regarding the church at Laodicea:

"You say, 'I am rich; I have acquired wealth and do not need a thing.' But you do not realise that you are wretched, pitiful, poor, blind and naked." (Revelation 3:17-18)

This church's view of itself was one of self-sufficiency. It had acquired material wealth and no doubt felt very prosperous. The church probably thought it had come into its inheritance, but Jesus saw otherwise. He saw that it was spiritually poor.

Today, we can have our programs, services, outpouring meetings and revivals (with a small "r") and yet not realise just how insufficient we are. We can give the appearance of an incredible amount of activity that looks "spiritual" on the surface, but is actually operating independently from God's will because He never sanctioned it. We are truly effective on the earth when we listen carefully to what God is saying and doing and then say and do the same things. That is when we begin to realise the fullness of our divine inheritance – as God empowers our actions in accordance with His will.

The same that is true of the Church is also true for us as individuals. Many have committed their lives to Christ and look forward to being with Him in heaven after they die. This is an amazing part of our inheritance in Him. But what about our lives on earth right now? How is that inheritance being manifest now?

In the book of Ephesians the apostle Paul writes of a twofold inheritance that is ours, right now:

"Blessed be the God and Father of our Lord Jesus Christ, who has blessed us with every spiritual blessing in the heavenly places in Christ." (Ephesians 1:3 NKJV)

"...the eyes of your understanding being enlightened; that you may know what is the hope of His calling, what are the riches of the glory of His inheritance in the saints." (Ephesians 1:18 NKJV)

It is clear from these scriptures that the blessing of God is not just for the future – that we will be spiritually blessed when we enter heaven – but it is powerfully present and active now, as we live here on earth. If then, we have been promised these blessings, it begs the question: are we receiving the fullness of them? And if not, why not?

I am certain that one reason many believers do not live in the full blessing of God is that they are unaware of the full scope of that blessing. They are unsure exactly what they have inherited as co-heirs with Christ and as such are failing to experience more of His dynamic life and power.

It is recorded that when slavery was abolished in the United States some slave owners continued to secure the services of their slaves by means of a very simple deception – they just didn't tell the slaves that they were free. Because the slaves knew no better, they accepted the status quo and continued with their labour. The most effective means of keeping someone from something is simply to avoid telling them about it. This is why Satan expends so much effort trying to darken people's minds and obscure the truth. It prevents the light of revelation from entering and greatly minimises our expectation of the supernatural.

What aspects of our inheritance then, should we remind ourselves of? I offer a few keys:

Inheritance is through relationship

God's desire has always been to enjoy fellowship with a people who would rule His creation in accordance with His heart. We could say that this desire and intention of God is the "big picture" of our inheritance. The more time we spend alone with God, simply being with Him and enjoying His presence, the more we will "absorb" and understand how He has empowered us to do what He desires us to do. The more time we spend in God's presence the more we receive our Father's affirmation of our sonship and identity and the less we strive for the affirmation of man. David said that the one thing that he sought was to dwell in the house of the Lord and gaze upon His beauty (Psalm 27:4). He was aware that as he did so he would again know the Lord's affirmation.

Our inheritance is the Kingdom

Experiencing the Father's love and affirmation prepares us for the second important aspect of our inheritance, participating in God's Kingdom:

"Then the King will say to those on his right, 'Come, you who are beloved by My Father; take your inheritance, the Kingdom prepared for you since the creation of the world.'" (Matthew 25:34).

The immediate context of these words relates to, "...when the Son of Man comes in His glory" (Matthew 25:31). But Jesus made it abundantly clear that His followers are to proclaim and demonstrate the Kingdom now, as Jesus said in Matthew 10:7-8:

"As you go, preach this message, 'The Kingdom of heaven is near or at hand, meaning you can reach out and touch it!' Heal the sick, raise the dead, cleanse those who have leprosy, drive out demons. Freely you have received, freely give.'"

Receive to give

A central principle of inheritance is that what is received is to be passed on. We receive what someone else has worked and paid the price for. In turn, we work for what we can pass on to others. I have spent years contending in prayer for manifestations of God's glory to break out in the UK as they have in places like Africa and India and God promised that my prayers would be answered. We saw part of that answer when what was planned as a week of meetings at the Ignited Church in Lakeland, Florida in April of 2008, turned into what became known as the "Lakeland Outpouring", with meetings every day and every night for months. I went to one of the early meetings and pressed in for the anointing I believed God wanted to impart.

On arriving back home the Holy Spirit fell in Dudley – so intensely that a similar pattern occurred and it became known as the "Dudley Outpouring". We hosted meetings every night for six months and during this time over 30,000 people came and received their own impartation of anointing and took it back to their churches and many nations around Europe.

People who went to Lakeland received another dimension

of their inheritance as they entered into worship, saw God's glory manifest, were healed or received prayer for impartation. But as I said when I spoke at Ignited Church in Florida on one occasion, God's intention is not that we keep our inheritance to ourselves. We are to use what we have received – which for me, meant going back home to arrange meetings where God could do what He did at Lakeland. At the very first meeting more than 1,000 people turned up. For many, their faith had been stirred; they prayed for others with a greater boldness and confidence, especially, for un-churched people and saw miracles, signs and wonders explode in their towns, cities and marketplaces.

Pressing in

There are often moments in our Christian lives when we get a glimpse of what God has for us and this should motivate us to press in for more. Often God will give us a taste of something that can be found only if we pursue a deeper experience of His presence. At times like these we need to intentionally pursue the things of God.

Such a moment happened to me in July 1994. At that time I had heard about a move of God in Toronto, Canada, which if I'm honest hadn't really impressed me. But news of what was happening in Toronto came at a time when I was experiencing a growing dissatisfaction and spiritual restlessness with the church and ministry I was involved in. During this time an Associate Pastor's role had opened up and I was due to be inducted into a Baptist Charismatic Church.

One of the last things I did was hand over the house groups I was responsible for. A meeting had been arranged where I was to say my farewell. However, God had a completely different agenda for that evening. As my friend Rudi Losch began to pray he started speaking in tongues and the whole atmosphere in the room changed. Steve Johnson, the church administrator stood up, looked over to Rudi and immediately fell under the presence of the Holy Spirit. Two of the ladies present saw what was taking place and began weeping. While all this continued I spontaneously fell to the floor holding my stomach, feeling as if I was going to explode and then I began to laugh, lifting my legs in air and peddling as if I was riding a bicycle. This whole experience lasted for three hours.

Never in my life had I experienced anything like this. I had been exposed to a completely different realm of the Spirit and had no map or compass to help me understand what God was doing in us. All I knew was that Jesus' presence had come very close to us and we were all overwhelmed. Still weighed down by the heavy presence of God I crawled along the ground to the telephone and called the other leader, Mark Edwards. All I could tell Mark was, "The Holy Spirit has come." From 11.30pm that night until around 1.30am in the morning, around forty members of the church visited Rudi's house. I remember someone saying to each person who came through the door, "God's got buckets tonight, not thimbles!" As they did so I felt God prompt me to act out throwing an imaginary "bucket of blessing" over the person. As I did, to my astonishment they would fall down, laugh, weep or dance.

After that night I never did leave to become Associate Minister of the Baptist church. God had visited us and all I could do was press in for more. Within a week, together with Mark Edwards and another friend, David Linnington, I was on a flight to Toronto to go and visit the Airport Vineyard Church (now Toronto Airport Christian Fellowship). I was suddenly very eager to learn as much as I could about what God was currently doing. It was to be the first of many visits and we would develop lasting relationships with John and Carol Arnott and Steve and Sandra Long.

The fact that we can receive freely, with no reluctance to give on God's part, does not mean that we should wait passively for our inheritance, as someone might wait for a cheque to come through the post from the family solicitor. When Moses died, Joshua, as the nation's new leader, inherited the land promised by God to Israel. But Joshua was told three times to be strong and courageous, suggesting that there would be trials ahead. We are to hold on to God's promises, imitating "those who through faith and patience inherit what has been promised" (Hebrews 6:12).

Even while we are pressing in, exercising faith and patience in order to receive the fullness of our inheritance, we can give out of what we have already received. Indeed, this is one of the keys to receiving more – being faithful with a little.

The apostle Paul's life suggests that entering fully into our inheritance may be a prolonged process, perhaps involving three distinct stages. These can be identified as visitation, destiny and commissioning.

Visitation, destiny and commissioning

There are many accounts in Scripture where a visitation has

opened up the way for a person to take hold of the plan God has for their life. It is this plan that I call "destiny" – fulfilling that which God has purposed for our lives. Once we have a revelation of our destiny in God, then we can be commissioned by Him to begin to live it out.

It was after that initial visitation and the subsequent journey to Toronto that God began to open up His plan and purpose in my life. It took place over an eighteen-month period as I continued to press in and take hold of all that God had for my life. To define "pressing in", this included regular times of prayer where I would simply aim to spend time in God's presence, seeking His face, prolonged periods of fasting, and culminating in a three-day silence and solitude retreat. After much seeking, it was at the end of those three days that God spoke clearly to my heart.

I had concluded my retreat and was preparing to leave the centre. I remember packing all my belongings and walking out of the room, in one sense a little disappointed because I had anticipated that surely this would be a time God would reveal His purposes to me. Though I was leaving with a deep sense of peace and a deeper knowledge of God's presence, I was still unclear regarding His plans for my future. As I turned to close the door of my room behind me, however, I clearly heard a voice say, "Come back here and I will show you what you will spend the rest of your life doing."

This voice was audible. It was like there was a person standing in my room, inviting me to go back in. I stepped back into the room and as I did so, I was overwhelmed by God's presence. The only words I can find to describe it are that it was like a warm oil being poured over my body, surrounding me, enveloping me. I was consumed and overwhelmed by the glory of God's presence. Then God spoke to me and said, "You were made for revival fire and I am giving you a revival spirit. It is a call to seek my presence. It is a call to deep purity. It is a call to fulfil the Matthew 28 commission. It is a call that will separate you from the ordinary to be a carrier of revival, and it is a fire that burns within your heart and will sustain you. This will be the working out of the vision: worship will be the foundation upon which you build. You will set before my people intercession as a lifestyle. You will teach them through the Word and through impartation of the anointing of the Holy Spirit how to minister. You will develop teams that will travel the world with this anointing. Healing and deliverance will be central to the preaching of the Gospel and you will set up centres of revival in the nation and the nations."

All this came as a gradual unfolding as God revealed His heart to me in His presence. At the end of this time I turned to Acts 26:16 and read,

"Now get up and stand on your feet. I have appeared to you to appoint you as a servant and as a witness of what you have seen and will see of me. I will rescue you from your own people and from the Gentiles. I am sending you to them to open their eyes and turn them from darkness to light, and from the power of Satan to God, so that they may receive forgiveness of sins and a place among those who are sanctified by faith in me."

From that initial visitation and continuing to press into God, He began to reveal more of His destiny for my life. All the things that were spoken to me on that day in 1998 we have seen established in the Apostolic Resource Centre in Dudley, which is the home of Revival fires.

I believe that every encounter with the supernatural realm should equip us to establish something upon the earth that corresponds to the pattern of heaven. These are not just experiences, but invitations to co-Labour with God and see the Kingdom of heaven come on earth.

Commissioning

Having received both the visitation and then the unfolding of God's destiny for my life over a period of a number of months, there came a time when the church that we were part of recognised this call upon my life. The apostolic oversight of the church, Dave Day of Bridge Ministries, laid hands on Sharon and me and commissioned us to set up the ministry of Revival Fires. Such a commissioning releases a new dimension of authority into our lives and gives recognition to the call of God operating in our lives. It makes a proclamation concerning that which we are about to fulfil.

We can see this in the life of Jesus when, in Matthew 3:17 God spoke from heaven and gave His stamp of approval saying, "This is my Son, whom I love; with Him I am well pleased." At that point Jesus was released to begin His earthly ministry. We see a similar thing happen to Paul in the book of Acts. Acts 9:3-4 recounts Paul's visitation:

"As he neared Damascus on his journey, suddenly a light from heaven flashed around him. He fell to the ground and heard a voice say to him, 'Saul, Saul, why do you persecute me?'"

Paul then entered into an open heaven experience as the presence of Jesus appeared with him. The Lord told Paul,

"Now get up and go into the city, and you will be told what you must do." (Acts 9:6)

The visitation happened in order to prepare him for increased revelation: the revelation that he later wrote about in his letter to the church in Galatia.

In a separate part of town a believer called Ananias had a vision in which the Lord instructed him to go and visit Paul at a particular address. He was to minister healing to Paul in order to restore his sight. God also revealed to Ananias his plans for Paul's life:

"This man is my chosen instrument to proclaim my name to the Gentiles and their kings and to the people of Israel." (Acts 9:15)

We read that,

"Then Ananias went to the house and entered it. Placing his hands on Saul, he said, 'Brother Saul, the Lord—Jesus, who appeared to you on the road as you were coming here—has sent me so that you may see again and be filled with the Holy Spirit.'"

It was after this encounter that Paul – who had been called Saul up until that point – had his name changed by God, just as Jacob had had his name changed to Israel (Prince of God) after a life-transforming encounter with Him (Genesis 35:1-15). Jesus also changed Simon Bar-Jonah's name to Peter (Matthew 16:16-18). A visitation from God inevitably leads us to experience a deeper revelation that confirms our identity and relationship with God.

During his time in Damascus Paul learned of his destiny and he immediately began to preach about Jesus. However, after a brief visit to Jerusalem he spent fourteen years in Tarsus before Barnabas sent for him to come to Antioch, where they taught together. It was here that Paul was commissioned.

"While they were worshipping the Lord and fasting, the Holy Spirit said, 'Set apart for me Barnabas and Paul for the work to which I have called them.' So after they had fasted and prayed, they placed their hands on them and sent them off." (Acts 13:2-3)

A double portion

There is perhaps no better way of ending this discussion of the "big picture" of our inheritance than by quoting part of Isaiah's prophecy of the restoration of Israel's inheritance in Isaiah 61:7:

"Instead of their shame my people will receive a double portion, and instead of disgrace they will rejoice in their inheritance; and so they will inherit a double portion in their land, and everlasting joy will be theirs."

When He went to the synagogue, Jesus quoted an earlier part

of this prophecy and applied it to Himself. As God's first-born Son, Jesus inherited a double portion, and the riches of His inheritance are found in us, God's children, as we proclaim and demonstrate the Kingdom.

Having looked at the big picture, we now narrow the focus to consider two ways in which our inheritance might operate. We first discuss the prophetic flow, and in particular the "seer anointing". Then we will look at the role of miracles in the extension of God's Kingdom.

The prophetic flow

The prophetic gift is evident and active throughout all of Scripture. There are numbers of good books that tackle the rationale for and correct use of the prophetic gift in ministry, so I will not attempt to add to that here. What I do want to do is speak about the main types of prophetic flow. The Old Testament uses two main words to speak about the prophetic flow. First there is the naba[1] – a Hebrew word meaning the "bubbling up" of the Spirit of God within us so that we begin to prophesy. The word literally means, "to speak under the influence of a divine Spirit". Second there is roeh[2] meaning to "see or perceive".

A roeh is a prophet or seer – the imagery alludes to someone for whom a curtain has been drawn back or a door opened in the spiritual realm and who sees for the first time something that has always been there, but which has now been revealed. Much of the prophetic operating in churches has been naba in nature, but I believe that God wants to raise up many more who can increasingly flow in the roeh gift.

The Seer anointing

This ability to see and perceive what is taking place in the heavenly realms as God's will is enacted aptly describes the seer anointing. Those who can flow in it learn to communicate what has been seen there. We know that God's will has always been to bless man, but if we are to co-operate fully with Him in the extension of His Kingdom, then it is helpful to know how God wishes to release His blessing today, at this moment.

Or, put another way: we can gain "information" from the Bible about God's Kingdom in heaven – for example, that there is no death, mourning, crying or pain there – but what measure of this can we expect to see reproduced on earth today? This is why the prophetic seer anointing is so vital in the Church today – it enables us to come into alignment with God's desires for His people, right now, and to move with faith to see His will come to pass on earth.

The first seer we see in Scripture is God Himself. After God created the natural light by which man sees, He then conveyed to Adam that he possessed the gift of being able to see and perceive. One of Adam's first tasks was to name all the animals God had created. We have already noted how God often changes a person's given name to a name more appropriate to their destiny in Him. I tend to think that God was allowing Adam to practice his "seer" gift by selecting appropriate names for the animals – and the words he spoke over those creatures have stood the test of time. God could have easily named all the animals Himself if He had wanted to, but this is a good example of how God's heart has always been for man to co-labour with

Him in order to bring about His will upon the earth.

John tells us that Jesus knew what was in the heart of man. He was a seer. In Revelation, the eyes of the ascended Jesus are described as being like blazing fire, penetrating, seeing all things. Elsewhere in Scripture we read that, "the eyes of the Lord range throughout the earth to strengthen those whose hearts are fully committed to him" (2 Chronicles 16:9). The Bible also teaches us that, "the Lord does not see as man sees; for man looks at the outward appearance, but the Lord looks at the heart " (1 Samuel 16:9 NKJV).

I believe that God is saying to us, "I am going to give you a seer gift. I want to give you something of Myself because I am the Greatest Seer."

A Forerunner anointing

The seer anointing brings with it a "forerunner anointing", as exemplified by John the Baptist, of whom the angel Gabriel declared in Luke 1:17:

"And he will go on before the Lord, in the spirit and power of Elijah to make ready a people prepared for the Lord."

John's testimony about Jesus was,

"I saw the Spirit come down from heaven as a dove and remain on him. And I myself did not know him, but the one who sent me to baptize with water told me, 'The man on whom you see the Spirit come down and remain is the one who will baptize with the Holy Spirit.'"

We are constantly preparing for Jesus and for Him to visit us and even make us into a habitation for His glory. We need the prophetic, forerunner anointing to keep reminding us about our need to prepare.

Miracles

Paul teaches us that the Father, "has rescued us from the dominion of darkness and brought us into the Kingdom of the Son he loves" (Colossians 1:13). But if God's purposes are to be fulfilled, then we are not simply to live in this Kingdom, but to participate in its extension, to co-operate with Jesus in destroying the devil's work. Jesus' Kingdom is a supernatural Kingdom and our lives should exhibit the supernatural: signs, wonders and miracles.

It is often asked, "Why are these things not seen more often, especially in our culture?" Could it be that the enemy has blinded the minds not only of unbelievers but also of Christians? I put it like this: unbelief resides in every area of our lives where faith is not present.[3] So, like Israel, often we are unable to receive what God has promised us because of our unbelief. Has the message we have heard become of no value to us, because we have not combined it with faith?

I recall one of our early Crusades in a city called Alipadur in India. We were teaching a healing seminar – something we ask everyone who accompanies us to attend – and while I was speaking I began to see a glowing light hovering over a woman who was bent over with a terrible curvature of the spine. I stopped speaking and asked some ladies near her to carry her to the front of the meeting, since she was unable to move about freely herself. I prayed for her and placed my hand on her back at the spot where I had seen the glowing light. As I did so, a loud crack resonated around the room and numbers of people were standing on their chairs, peering to see what was happening. The sound was like someone had taken a dry stick and snapped it. What took place then was truly amazing as this woman stood up straight and, as she did so, grew a whole four inches as her back came into proper alignment. This one miracle charged the whole room with a tremendous excitement that God was about to move in miraculous power in their city.

In other crusades in India we have seen the lame walk, the blind see, the deaf hear and many creative miracles. We have recorded healings for the following: brain tumours, stomach growths, neck growths, tumours on backs, breast tumours and tumours in lymph glands. There has been deliverance from demons, hearing has been restored, eyes completely healed, swellings going down, improved mobility of limbs, mouths opened from dumb spirits, deliverance from oppression and fear, and many miracles where barrenness was healed! Insomnia, diabetes, kidney stones, fevers, sickness and kidneys have all miraculously healed and we have seen children walking who were paralysed from birth.

Truly God's power is able to be manifest where we are committed to seeing what He is doing in heaven first, and then co-operating with the Holy Spirit to enact that on earth.

Doors

A miracle is a door, an entry point, where the natural realm is suspended enabling us to penetrate this spiritual realm where the rule and reign of heaven, the Kingdom of light, breaks in and dispels the kingdom of darkness. This is what happened when Peter spoke the word of healing to the crippled beggar who had asked John and him for money in Acts 3:7: "Instantly the man's feet and ankles became strong." As the man walked along with Peter and John, praising God, many people came up to see what had happened. This gave Peter the opportunity to preach the gospel and it resulted in many new believers.

We read that the twelve handed over certain tasks to other disciples so that they could give their "attention to prayer and the ministry of the word" (Acts 6:4). While prayer, study and the proclamation of God's word are vitally important, the apostles clearly expected this to go hand in hand with a demonstration of the Gospel.

I believe the Church is entering in to a new season where it will not just be plausible words but demonstrations of the Spirit's power that will cause a breaking in of the Kingdom of heaven. I believe that God is calling us to ask Him to anoint our eyes with eye salve so that we can see. This will result in the suspension of the natural realm so that there will be a new release of the Spirit where He reveals the unseen realm and so prepares us to have a continuous encounter with the supernatural power of the Kingdom of heaven.

Chapter 4
Is The Church Ready?

In this season I believe that there is a door in heaven that God has opened in order to pour out the miraculous and supernatural on His Church. Those who earnestly desire this and are ready to co-operate with whatever God tells them to do will see unparalleled power and blessing to spread the Gospel and usher in God's Kingdom. But I ask the question: is the contemporary Church ready to take advantage of such an open door in heaven? Are we eager to call on heaven's resources so that we become more effective in our proclamation and demonstration of the Gospel? Is God causing us to trust less in our own efforts and be less satisfied with the number of disciples made, people healed, and poor helped? Is He undermining our sense of self-sufficiency? Have we opened heaven's door on earth for which we, as gatekeepers, are responsible? Or has it remained closed in our lives?

The closed door on earth

I believe that in many places the door of the Church has been closed to heaven. The access point on the earth has been closed to the glory of the supernatural because pastors have been frightened of the supernatural realms and have taught their people to fear it too – even if they have done so inadvertently. In fact, the Church, especially in the West, has inherited a legacy of being numb and closed off to the supernatural – unlike other places such as China, India and Africa where the spiritual world is view and spoken of very differently. In the West, very often we do not like what we do not know how to control. If we cannot control something, we tend to fear it and try to avoid it.

This has, unfortunately, created a culture within the Church where leaders find much more comfort putting their trust in programs to grow their churches or see the sick healed. We want five easy steps, three jumps or twelve hurdles to overcome our problems. Exercising a simple formula is much more appealing to us than trusting God and asking the Holy Spirit to take control.

Often it is healthy to step back from what we have been doing and question whether it is still relevant to God's current purposes. Just because something has worked in the past, does not mean that we should keep on doing it now. The Holy Spirit is always on the move and we need to learn to be fluid and flexible, following His lead.

Take our worship in church as an example. We may have a great band and gifted leaders, but what good is it if we just have forty-five minutes of songs that touch our souls and make us feel good? There is nothing wrong, of course, with singing and feeling good – but how is that different from the pleasure that performers on any stage produce? We need to be asking, how is our worship connecting us to the reality of the spiritual realm, where we enter the heavenly courts of worship and see the things that God is wanting to do? This is just one example of how we need to remain aligned with the Spirit, but it applies to every aspect of our life and ministry.

The church at Laodicea was very satisfied with its situation: "I am rich; I have acquired wealth and do not need a thing" (Revelation 1:17). But we know that this opinion was not shared by Jesus: "You do not realise that you are wretched, poor, pitiful, blind and naked." What a verdict!

Jesus' invitation

Jesus' intention, however, in delivering this verdict was not to condemn the church, but to encourage them to accept His invitation and offer of help:

"I counsel you to buy from Me gold refined in the fire, so that you can become rich; and white clothes to wear, so that you can cover your shameful nakedness; and salve to put on your eyes, so that you can see. Those whom I love I rebuke and discipline. So be earnest and repent; Here I am! I stand at the door and knock. If anyone hears My voice and opens the door, I will come in and eat with him, and he with Me." (Revelation 3:18-20)

I believe that the door on earth has been closed to heaven, but God is asking us to open the door – to open ourselves up to His supernatural invasion in a new way. Notice here that although Jesus is addressing an entire church, He goes on to say, "If anyone hears My voice and opens the door…". I believe it needs only one person, fully yielded to God, who is prepared to open the door to what God wants to spark the start of a revival. Let me be clear that I am not speaking about anyone usurping the authority of those serving in leadership, but we each have a divine right to open the door so that heaven can come in. The exalted Lord Jesus Christ, the Almighty One, stands at the door. Jesus does not gate crash; He comes in when invited. "If any one hears My voice and opens the door, I will come in and eat with him, and he with Me." What a great promise Jesus makes to us.

Seated on the throne of God

What will happen when we humble ourselves, repent of our self-sufficiency and ask Jesus to take over the running of our lives? I believe that the Kingdom of God will come with great power.

"To him who overcomes, I will give the right to sit with Me on My throne, just as I overcame and sat down with My Father on His throne." (Revelation 3:21)

When we are "sitting" in heavenly places with God, we are no longer battling or striving. We are seated in a place of incredible favour with the King, in agreement with the decrees of Almighty God. When a king issues a decree, he can do it seated on his throne. He doesn't need to stand up to assert his authority — he can exercise his authority from a place of rest, whilst sitting down. Jesus overcame and sat down with His Father on His throne and Paul proclaims the same truth about those who are in Christ: "And God raised us up with Christ and seated us with Him in the heavenly realms in Christ Jesus" (Ephesians 2:6).

In Revelations 4:1, John continues, "After this I looked, and there before me was a door standing open in heaven." After what? After the door had been opened into the church. Jesus had stood outside the door, knocking, wanting to come in. Now He comes in and eats with those who opened the door, in fellowship with them. When the door on earth is opened, God has a place where His Spirit may abide, where His glory may be seen. Eventually, as prophesied by Habakkuk, "the earth will be filled with the knowledge of the glory of the Lord, as the waters cover the sea"(Habakkuk 2:14).

Restoring honour and value to the Church

I believe the Church is going to come to a place where it is valued once again, instead of being marginalised or ridiculed. A fire is beginning to burn that people will see and be drawn toward. This fire will be ignited in any church that takes the counsel of God and flows with it.

"Nations will come to your light, and kings to the brightness of your dawn." (Isaiah 60:3)

The story of Bartimaeus can be seen as a parable of what God is doing in the Church. The name Bartimaeus means "son of value", but instead of being valued or honoured, Bartimaeus had to beg for his bread (Mark 10:46-7 and 50-52):

"A blind man, Bartimaeus (that is, the son of Timaeus), was sitting by the roadside begging. When he heard that it was Jesus of Nazareth he began to shout, 'Jesus, Son of David, have mercy on me'... He jumped to his feet and came to Jesus. 'What do you want Me to do for you?' Jesus asked him. The blind man said, 'Rabbi, I want to see.' 'Go,' said Jesus, 'your faith has healed you.' Immediately he received his sight and followed Jesus along the road."

Jesus gave Bartimaeus value by giving him eyes to see. No longer did he need to beg. He stepped into what God had already spoken about his life: "Bartimaeus, you are a son of value." His eyes were opened and he saw Jesus, the Light of the World. Wouldn't you like that to be your vision, not just once, but on a daily basis? Such vision is required if we are to enter fully into our inheritance.

Stepping into our inheritance

In later chapters we discuss some of the sources of revelation. But whatever revelation we get, it must point us to Jesus. We must never be distracted from the full-on, eyes-wide-open revelation of Jesus. The seer anointing is what the Church is missing. When a dentist touches a nerve we tend to wake up pretty quickly. I believe that God is touching the nerve of the Church and prompting us to respond: "I have lived as a beggar long enough; I want eyes to see." God has been showing us the poverty of our own lives and the life of the Church. Renewal and revival are restoring the vision that the Father has stored up for us.

I believe that the enemy has sought to kill and destroy the desire and ability of believers to see the realities of the supernatural realm on a regular basis. God wants to touch our eyes so that we catch glimpses of glory, leading us to live life fully engaged in the supernatural realm.

Entering into the supernatural realms

Once the door on earth is open, revelation comes very easily, because heaven is not closed. God does not say, "Knock on My door!" He says, "I am knocking on your door." When we open our door, we find a corresponding door open in heaven. In line with Jesus' promise to Nathanael, noted earlier, angels will ascend and descend between earth and heaven, going to and fro in fulfilling their commission to serve the Church – "those who will inherit salvation" (Hebrews 1:14).

Seeing the realities of heaven

"And the voice I had first heard speaking to me like a trumpet said 'Come up here, and I will show you what must take place after this.'" (Revelation 4:16)

John's record of what he saw includes a throne with someone sitting on it with the appearance of jasper and carnelian. A rainbow resembling an emerald encircled the throne, from which came lightning and thunder. He also saw twenty-four elders on twenty-four other thrones and seven blazing lamps, the seven Spirits of God.

As we continue to read through Revelation 4 and 5 we see the elders, the living creatures, the angels and then the whole of creation gathered around the throne bowing down and worshipping. Read this passage again for yourself now. As you read it, my prayer is that your eyes will be anointed with eye salve to enable you to see the realities of heaven, so that you can move on from relying on or falling back on your own natural abilities and begin to see what God can do!

A Prayer:

Pray the following prayer with me now:

"Father, thank you that your perspective is different to the way that I see things. I respond to your invitation and ask You for eye salve for my eyes so that I can see. Lord, I pray right now that the eyes of my heart may be enlightened that I might know the hope to which you call me and know the glorious inheritance that you have put within me, and know that the all-surpassing power that raised Jesus from the dead is working in me. Lord, I ask that I might live in this realm of the Spirit, having my spiritual senses activated so that I may look not only on the things that are easily seen, but the spiritual things that are unseen. I ask this in Jesus' name. Amen."

Chapter 5
An Open Door
Lifestyle

In this chapter I offer several principles that if applied will lead to living an "open door lifestyle". When embraced and lived out together they will position us to receive God's supernatural blessing.

Prayer

The prayers of the early Church welcomed the invasion of heaven on earth. We will continue to see the coming of God's Kingdom on earth demonstrated in dramatic ways when we as believers choose to open the door. But our desire is, of course, that the door on earth be continually open, and that the "everlasting doors" would open as wide as possible so that the King of Glory would come in (Psalm 24:9). This requires a lifestyle in which prayer plays a major role.

The importance of prayer in the life of the early Church, as in Jesus' life here on earth, is seen very clearly in the book of Acts. In Chapter 4 Peter and John were forbidden to continue proclaiming the name of Jesus Christ and were put in prison for the night. After their release, the church prayed, "Lord consider their threats and enable your servants to speak Your word with great boldness" (Acts 4:29). God's answer was immediate in verse 31: "After they prayed, the place where they were meeting was shaken. And they were all filled with the Holy Spirit and spoke the word of God boldly."

In Acts Chapter 10 we read how God's Kingdom was extended to the Gentiles through Peter's ministry. We meet Cornelius, a Roman centurion, who, "gave generously to those in need and prayed to God regularly" (Acts 10:2). One day, while he was praying, God sent an angel to him. The angel told Cornelius that he was to send for Peter and he told him where Peter could be found (Acts 10:4-6).

An open vision

On the following day Peter went up on to the roof to pray. As he did he fell into a trance and had a vision that was to change his theology. He saw heaven open and a sheet being let down which contained all kinds of animals, reptiles and birds. When the Lord told him to kill and eat these creatures Peter was shocked. As a good Jew he had never eaten anything declared under the Old Covenant regulations to be impure or unclean. But the Lord rebuked him for calling impure things that God had made clean.

This vision was seen three times[3] and the sheet was then

taken back to heaven. While Peter was still pondering what the vision meant, he was told by the Spirit to go down to meet the delegation that was coming from Cornelius and to go back with them. When he arrived at Cornelius' house Peter began to proclaim the Gospel and as he did so he was interrupted as the Holy Spirit was poured out on his hearers, who began to speak in tongues and praise God.

In Acts 12:5 Peter was in prison awaiting trial, "...but the church was earnestly praying to God for him." As Peter was sleeping he had an open heaven experience. An angel struck Peter on his side to waken him and told him to get up. The chains fell off Peter's wrists and he and the angel walked past the guards and out through the prison door which opened by itself.

In Acts Chapter 16 Paul and Silas, having been severely flogged, were thrown into prison and their feet were put into stocks. What was their response? At about midnight Paul and Silas were praying and singing hymns to God. What was God's response? Suddenly there was such a violent earthquake that the foundations of the prison were shaken. At once all of the prison doors flew open and everybody's chains came loose. Seeing this and no doubt fearing for his life, the jailer asked, "Sirs, what must I do to be saved?"(Acts 16:30).

This was an opportunity not to be missed! Verse 31 records their response: "Believe in the Lord Jesus, and you will be saved – you and your household ... And the jailer was filled with joy because he had come to believe in God – he and his whole family." (Acts 16:31-34)

In answer to our prayers, heaven can be manifested and God can bless us in the most dramatic manner. We also see that God's ultimate purpose is that we then become a source of blessing to others.

Humility

In the parable that Jesus told concerning the Pharisee and the tax collector going up to the temple to pray, the Pharisee was full of pride and a sense of his own importance, probably thinking: "I am so much better than the tax collector." The tax collector, on the other hand, knew that there were things wrong in his life and asked God for mercy. Jesus said that the one who humbles himself is the one who will be justified and exalted. The principle here is clear: when we show humility and recognise our need of God, we receive from Him. The tax collector knew that he needed to receive forgiveness. Often we know that we need to experience a greater fullness of the Spirit, so we need to humble ourselves before God.

Some years ago I went to speak at a church. When I arrived, I first went into a side room to pray with the ministry team before the meeting. There I saw a little glass on a shelf and a large bin that could be used for waste. A question then came into my mind: "How thirsty for the Holy Spirit are the people? What measure would they select if the Holy Spirit was like water poured out? Would they want a glassful or a dustbin poured over them?" During the prayer time that followed I saw a vision of a waterfall with water rushing down, and people enjoying themselves in God going with the current flow of the river.

When the evening meeting started and I got up to speak, I knew that I had to bring the glass and the dustbin onto the stage.

I fetched them in and then asked the people, "How much of the Holy Spirit do you want tonight?" Before I knew it, people were coming out and taking hold of the bin. At one point I counted four people with their heads in the bin – demonstrating how thirsty they were for more of God's Spirit!

I had said very little, but people were now coming down to the front and jumping in. One very polite, smartly dressed, man said, "Excuse me Trevor, could I get inside the bin?" I told him that he could do whatever he wanted. So he climbed inside the bin and as he did so he started to shake. Then, as his shaking increased, the bin fell over and he rolled around the room.

Afterwards I asked him what was happening to him spiritually. He told me, "You know, all my life people have put their expectations on me. Ever since I was small, I have always done what everyone expected me to do. You wouldn't believe this but I have a PhD in Psychology and lecture at a local university. But tonight it was as though God took me down the rapids, and as I went down the rapids I could see all the stuff that people had loaded on me, coming off. It was the most liberating experience I've ever had!"

Truly, a man who had humbled himself, had been transformed and greatly blessed!

Intimacy

When the anointing of the Holy Spirit comes, it causes the burden of other people's expectations to be shaken off and we see God's power in action. But opening ourselves up to the Holy Spirit's ministry also gives rise to intimacy.

1 Samuel 10:1 explains how God chose Saul to be the first king of Israel:

"Samuel took a flask of oil and poured it on Saul's head and kissed him, saying, 'Has not the Lord anointed you leader over his inheritance?'"

The flask would have contained a large amount of oil. When that much oil is poured on someone it makes a mess! Do we sometimes limit what the Holy Spirit wishes to do because it may be messy? Because we don't want to make a spectacle of ourselves? In fact, it is God who is making a spectacle of Himself. It is about Him, not us. Yet our cultural norms can stop us from really being ourselves – people who want to have an intimate relationship with Him.

When Samuel kissed Saul this signified the intimacy that comes through the anointing. Out of this comes destiny and calling – Saul was chosen to lead Israel. I believe that there is a "kiss of intimacy" that releases us into our destiny and calling, and it comes through the anointing and the pouring out of the Holy Spirit.

Obedience: our responsibility to the anointing

When Samuel had anointed Saul he told him that in Gibeah he would meet a group of prophets who would be prophesying, and that,

"The Spirit of the Lord will come upon you in power, and you will prophesy with them; and you will be changed into a different person." (1 Samuel 10:6)

When the anointing changes us, we do things we have not done before. When Saul met the prophets, "the Spirit of God came upon him in power, and he joined in the prophesying." This caused the people who knew him to ask, "What is this that has happened to the son of Kish? Is Saul also among the prophets?"

So Saul was a changed man, but how deep was the change? I have known people who have rolled on the floor and laughed with me, and have been incredibly anointed with the Holy Spirit, but are now no longer walking with God. I believe this is because they did not allow the anointing to ignite an ongoing process of change in them, whereby the Holy Spirit transformed them from one degree of glory to another.

Awareness

As we noted in the previous chapter, Jesus advised the church at Laodicea to buy eye salve so that they could see. Very often an important step to seeing is simply awareness or openness. If we are in a room where the windows and doors are closed and we feel a wind across our face or a sudden heat, what registers with us? Maybe nothing! Or maybe we think, "He makes His angels winds, and His servants flames of fire" (Hebrews 1:7). Being sensitive to the Holy Spirit at all times opens us up to seeing into the supernatural.

Several years ago, when we were holding meetings in Patna, India, we saw round, glowing balls of light. Having seen these on two nights, we decided on the following night to take photographs. When these were developed, they revealed all manner of orbs of light, some small and some large. It seemed that the biggest orbs were hovering on the people receiving prayer; they often had rainbow orbs appearing around their stomach area. Why would God do something like this? What is the purpose of it? I believe that God wants us more and more to see heavenly realities – to take a glimpse behind the veil into the realm of heaven, to take what I call flights of the Spirit.

Flights of the Spirit

I believe that sometimes these glimpses into the realm of heaven are simply designed to get our attention and ask God, "Lord, what are you saying to me through this? What is it that you want me to understand?" On other occasions – such as with the healings in Patna – I believe they are God giving us a clear insight into what He is busy doing now, as the balls of light indicated where He was healing people. On still other occasions they can enable us to influence the future, to help God's Kingdom expand on the earth.

More than a decade ago now, on 1st April 1999, we were convinced that God wanted us to buy what is now called the Grace Centre, but we had a planning application refused twice. Two weeks before the planning committee was due to meet again, we went away for a few day's break. One morning while we were praying, I saw in a vision right into the town council's meeting room. It was so vivid that I felt as if God had transported me there and placed me at the table. The full council was there and they were all speaking negatively about the building we wished to buy. In the vision I went around to each person saying, "No, be quiet, that is wrong, you are making that up, that is not true." Eventually I told the planning officer that it was time for him to speak. He stood up and said that the council should approve the planning application.

Two weeks later, when the council met, things happened much as I had seen them (except that I was not in the meeting!) Various members of the council started to speak, but then fell silent. Finally the planning officer proposed that the application be accepted and we were given planning permission.

Relationship

Much of this chapter has shown how you or I as individuals can ensure that we position ourselves in order to live under an open heaven or open door before God. But Jesus said that He would be present wherever two or three are gathered in His name, and it seems that the richest blessings often accompanies a like-minded gathering.

When I was at a Partners in Harvest conference in Hemel Hempstead, Sharon and I were sitting at a table having a meal with John and Carol Arnott. As we were talking I saw an angel with a sword come behind Carol. Suddenly she started to shake as the Spirit came upon her and she waved her arms like she was holding a sword. I told her that the angel of the Lord was giving the sword back to her. Some years earlier an angel had given her a sword that she had used to knight people, that is, release them into their calling and anointing. But I said that this was not a sword to knight with, but the sword of the victories of God. The anointing of God increased tangibly at that moment and I prophesied to Carol that her sword was going to be used to bring the victories of God to the earth, and that she should ask God to reveal the victories into which she should speak His Word.

We then went into the meeting and John suggested that I should speak that night instead of him. As I stood up to speak, an angel of healing came and began to pour out a river of healing on the carpet. Although perhaps only two or three people could see the river in the Spirit, many people were healed as they stepped into it.

One woman fell under the power of the Spirit and lay on the floor for three hours. Although she was petite, four men were needed to pick her up! She could not bend and so they had to slide her into the back of a people carrier to transport her back to her hotel. She had to be carried to her room and she stayed rigid until 8 o'clock the next morning. In that time she had an encounter where she entered into the throne room of God. Many other wonderful things happened in that meeting, but it all started with a few friends talking about God's presence and choosing to literally enter in deeper than ever.

Nurturing the seed

We know that God is, "able to do immeasurably more than all we ask or imagine, according to His power that is at work within us" (Ephesians 3:20). Yet God may need to draw our attention back continually to the immensity of that power. In Genesis 15:5 God promised Abraham that his offspring would be as numerous as the dust of the earth. Yet as the years passed, he remained childless and he asked God how the promise could possibly be fulfilled. God took him outside and told him to count the stars. Then he said to him, "So shall your offspring be."

We too have to trust God that the seed He has put in us, either individually or corporately, will mature. Mark's parable of the growing seed in Mark chapter 4 suggests that God's word, God's promise, the seed planted within our heart, will develop even when we are unaware that this is happening. That seed is your calling, destiny and purpose, which is the desires of your heart. In this early stage of development, the seed remains hidden, concealed.

But the same parable suggests that we have a part to play in ensuring that the seed grows into a mature plant. After the time of concealment, the plant first becomes visible as a blade or stalk. The time when we first come into a place of prominence is the time when we are most vulnerable! The softest of touches can destroy the blade and we need to be aware of becoming over sensitive to the opinions and criticisms of others.

The blade that survives becomes an ear. The place of vulnerability becomes the place of strength. The blade or stalk supports the ear in the same way that the support we give to one another at these vital growth points strengthens us at particular times in our lives.

The final stage in the plant's development is the full grain in the ear. The ultimate purpose in the time of concealment was to break through in order that a harvest might be produced. But the harvest does not come until the grain is ripe. Sometimes we can harvest too early. A farmer will go into a field, take an ear of corn, put it in his hands and smell it in order to know whether it is ripe. It is essential to understand the timings of God as He brings us into greater fruitfulness and maturity.

If we fail at any of these stages, what then? Well even a blade that has been trodden down can survive. As Paul said, as long as God is working within us we may be hard pressed but not crushed, struck down but not destroyed.

We have been visiting India for sixteen years and in that time we have come into contact with many people. We have constantly asked God which relationship would help us to fulfil the things that He has spoken into our lives. Where do we find the strengthening? Where will the ear become full? Fostering these relationships has been costly and sometimes we have seen no return. But, convinced of our calling, we pressed on.

Then in our eleventh year we met a group of leaders who I believed would open up the whole of the Northeast region of India. We regularly receive emails thanking us for coming and inviting us back again. But the emails from these leaders also contain news of what God is doing after we leave. They are saying that God is moving through them, the local leaders and others, after we leave. These last few years have seen follow-up teams planting churches and discipling new believers throughout the plains of the Northeast of India. We have also established Papa's House, a home for up to 30 girls and boys who would otherwise be living in abject poverty. Here they are loved, educated and given skills to succeed in life.

Let's remember and seek to nurture all of the truths we have discussed that will lead us into open door living, sensitive to the Holy Spirit and what He desires to do in us and through us.

Chapter 6
Angelic Visitations

In this present season, as God demonstrates His desire to manifest His presence in an ever-increasing way and make us more sensitive to the supernatural realm, there has been a growing increase in angelic activity. Often, when people begin talking about angels, their comments are treated with suspicion and scepticism, but the presence of angels on the earth should not be a surprise to anyone. There are numerous examples in Scripture of angels interacting with humans, whether that is to relay a message or guidance from God, provide protection or to give a glimpse into what is really happening in a situation from a heavenly perspective.

Many people – not just Christians – believe in angels. Often people will say, "Yes, I believe in angels," and then go on to qualify this statement by stating that they have a guardian angel who looks after them or their children. Many will have stories to back up this belief, of how they have been helped in extraordinary ways in times of need. This has certainly been my experience.

I remember on one of our visits to India we had arranged a visit to Agra to see the Taj Mahal. Sharon and I had arrived at Delhi railway station at 5:00am to catch the Taj Express. The pastor we were staying with had assigned an escort to put us on the train. However, this arrangement proved to be a tenuous one at best. It's hard to describe if you have never been there, but there is constantly a crowd of people thronging around the entrance to the station, all rushing in different directions going about their business. Then there are street traders trying to sell their wares, taxi drivers touting for business and unofficial porters keen to help you with your bags – for 100 rupees, of course.

In the midst of all this bedlam were two nervous people, Sharon and me, with our hand luggage and cameras in full view. To make matters worse, our escort instructed us to wait where we were on the street while he parked the car and then disappeared into the early morning crowd. After waiting 45 minutes for him to return I eventually realised we were on our own, with no idea of where to go, and to make matters worse we had become the focus of some very undesirable characters who had begun to close around us.

In the midst of all this, however, just as we were beginning to feel really vulnerable, an Indian man, smartly dressed in a blue suit, strode up to us through the crowd and asked us to follow him. Although he spoke in a very soft voice, his voice was, at once, commanding – and contrary to all my natural instincts regarding safety and falling into the hands of strangers, I found myself taking Sharon by the hand and falling in behind him as he led us away. We followed him down the street and he took us through a different entrance into the station and led us to our correct platform. He then opened the carriage door and ushered us onto the train.

At this moment, our original "escort" turned up and found us. I expressed my thanks to him for sending someone to guide us to the train, but he told us that he had not sent anyone and had been anxious for our safety. I immediately turned towards the man in the blue suit to speak to him, but he had disappeared. It was then that I realised God must have sent an angel to guard and direct us.

I'm sure many reading this will have their own testimonies of how God has provided angelic help in their lives. There is so much more to the ministry of angels, so let us consider some of these aspects. In looking at Jesus' life we see that they were present at all the major transitional events. As you read though Scripture it becomes evident that angels seem to function as door keepers who help believers transition into new spheres of ministry, provide safe passage as we travel, or provide protection in times of conflict. If this assistance was available to believers previously, then today we should anticipate the same kind of supernatural activity operating in and around our lives.

The nature of angels

Angels were ever-present in Jesus' life. They were in attendance at His birth, with Him in His temptation in the wilderness, present during His testing in the garden of Gethsemane, and there at His resurrection and ascension. Hebrews 1:14 teaches us that angels are dispatched to minister to and with believers today. We should, therefore, be open and alert to angelic visitations.

Angels are created beings who, according to Job 38:7, were in existence when the natural world was being created. It seems that a predetermined number of angels were created at that point. Subsequently, "When men began to increase in number on the earth and daughters were born to them, the sons of God [another term for angelic beings] saw that the daughters of men were beautiful, and they married any of them they chose." This was disorder, or a perversion of what God intended and so He moved to stop this activity. Incidentally, this passage indicates that although angels are spirit beings they can present themselves in human form.

This ungodly activity was a symptom of Satan's rebellion. I believe, as do many commentators, that Ezekiel's prophecy about the king of Tyre, that model of perfection, anointed as a guardian cherub, blameless since the day he was created until wickedness was found in him, refers to Satan (Ezekiel 28:12, 14, 15).

God's response to Satan's wickedness was to expel him from heaven: "Your heart became proud on account of your beauty, and you corrupted your wisdom because of your splendour. So I threw you to the earth" (Ezekiel 28:17). Then in Isaiah we read,

"You said in your heart, 'I will ascend to heaven; I will raise my throne above the stars of God; I will sit enthroned on the mount of assembly, on the utmost heights of the sacred mountain. I will ascend above the tops of the clouds; I will make myself like the Most High,' but you are brought down to the grave, to the depths of the pit." (Isaiah 14:13-15)

It appears that Satan infected one third of the angels and they too were cast to the earth. The other two thirds have remained loyal to God and carry out His commands:

"The Lord has established His throne in heaven, and His Kingdom rules over all. Praise the Lord, you His angels, you mighty ones who do His bidding, who obey His word." (Psalms 103:20)

Theologians differ as to whether all demons are fallen angels. We need not concern ourselves with this controversy; the essential point is that there is a spiritual army under Satan's command. This is why it is important to understand the role of those angels who are obedient to God, a role which was emphasised by the Church fathers.

The Church fathers

The historian Eusebius tells us that Clement of Alexandria, one of the early Church fathers, taught that there is a hierarchy in the angelic realm. He confirmed that angels appear to men and that they are not to be worshipped. Dionysus the Areopagite[4], a first century bishop of Athens, spoke of a three-fold hierarchy in which the first rank, those who dwell nearest to God, included Cherubim and Seraphim; the second contained Powers, Virtues and Dominions, and the third comprised Angels, Archangels and Principalities.

Augustine said that good angels were rewarded for their

obedience and perseverance and that they would never fail. The Council of Laodicea (AD 363-4) considered angels not as iconic figures (such as found in wall paintings or statues), but as living beings that visited the earth and that they should not be worshipped. In the Middle Ages, Thomas Aquinas (1225-1274) and John Duns Scotus (1265-1308) both spoke of angels as beings who could acquire and be infused with knowledge.

Some Reformation theologians sought to minimise the scope of the angelic realm. But both Luther and Calvin spoke vividly about angels, and in particular about fallen angels or demons. Throughout the Reformation there was no general agreement about the role of good or guardian angels. However, angelic beings have always been seen as having something to do with helping man to receive salvation.

Servants of God

The job of angels is to carry out the commands of God. Space does not permit a full discussion of their spheres of activity, but it is clear that angels have been involved in events of the greatest significance. Here is a summary of their spheres of activity:

- the completion of creation (Job 38:7)
- the giving of the Law (Galatians 3:19, Hebrews 2:2)
- the birth of Jesus (Luke 2:13)
- the temptation of Jesus (Matthew 4:11)
- the intercession of Jesus in Gethsemane (Luke 22:43)
- the resurrection (Matthew 28:2)
- the ascension (Acts 1:10)

• and they will attend Jesus when he comes in His glory (Matthew 25:31)

Angels and the Law

We have seen that angels were present when the Law was given. But the Bible goes further, telling us that the Law was "put into effect by angels" (Acts 7:53). What did Luke mean when he wrote this? The Law that God gave to Adam in Genesis 2:16-17 said, "You are free to eat from any tree in the garden; but you must not eat from the tree of the knowledge of good and evil, for when you eat of it you will surely die." When Adam sinned, access to the tree of life was blocked by cherubim and a flaming sword. Angels therefore put into effect the consequence of sin and Adam was barred from the tree of life.

Seeing angels

We may agree that angels can protect us, but some may wonder whether there is any advantage in seeing them. Balaam's experience would suggest that there is:

"Balaam got up in the morning, saddled his donkey and went with the princes of Moab. But God was very angry when he went, and the angel of the Lord stood in the road to oppose him." (Numbers 22:22)

The angel had a drawn sword in his hand, but Balaam did not see him. Fortunately for him, God in His mercy allowed his donkey to see the angel, so that she turned away, not once but three times, an action that saved Balaam's life.

When Jesus spoke to John on the island of Patmos He told him to write to the angels, the messengers, of the churches. Surely this is sufficient encouragement to us to be alert to the fact that an angel may want to be seen or heard by us. If we have this attitude, and assuming that we are walking with the Lord, if we see an angel, our response could be to ask, "What have you come to communicate to me?" Instead of being afraid we can trust God to speak to us in whatever way He deems appropriate.

Engaging with the unexpected

There have been many occasions when God has done what I did not expect Him to do, causing me to wonder what was happening. Before 2004 I had been privileged to have six or so angelic visitations, but then nothing happened for quite some time. In the Summer of 2004, in Anacortes, a town near Seattle, I was woken up one night by a presence. I just knew that there was someone in the room. I opened my eyes to see a twenty-foot tall angel in a golden robe, surrounded by a green aura. The angel told me to get out of bed. As I did so I became fully engaged with everything that was taking place. The angel said, "Hold out your hands" and as I did so the angel began to pour gold sovereigns into my hands. Then a map of the world appeared on the floor and I was told to go over to the map and pour the gold into whatever nation I wanted to. So I poured it all into North East India.

As I poured the gold sovereigns into the map, the gold became molten. Then bodily forms started to grow from where I was pouring the gold; they became like golden, molten, images. First there were children, then there were women, then there were men. As they grew, I saw that the children began to hand bowls of rice to the women, and the women began to hand them to the men. As the children gave out the bowls of rice, they were given sacks of rice, and as they continued to give it out a great sack appeared which covered the whole area. People came in their thousands to pick up the provision of the rice that was there. Then the angel was gone, the map was gone and the people who had been in the room were gone too. Wondering what the significance of this was, I wrote everything down.

Moving into our inheritance

The following year we were in the North East of India. We were feeding up to 1,500 people a day and 15,000 or more were gathering at our crusades. We had never seen anything like this before. In the three places that we visited, we probably saw 20,000 people come to Christ – predominantly Hindus. Since then we have continued with our feeding programme, mass meetings, and we have seen an incredible release of finance to support the ministry and outreach to the poor in that region.

We knew that we were called to North East India and had been following that call for a number of years. The angelic visitation was an encouragement for us to continue in this ministry. But I also believe that it was a prophetic sign, pointing to a greater measure of God's provision and of the increased fruitfulness to follow. I believe that for every follower of Jesus, angels can reveal more of the inheritance that we spoke of earlier and of the good works that God has prepared for us to do.

Ministering healing

In one of our mass meetings in 2005, I preached a message asking, "Do you need a shelter, a shrine or a Saviour who cleanses from sin?" Four thousand people came to Christ that night. Was that a result of the relevance of the message? Perhaps partly, but I believe it was also due to the appearance of an angel of healing who appeared during the meeting. When he came into the meeting and hovered over the crusade ground, the whole atmosphere changed; God's presence was there.

Earlier in the day God had told me, "Say to them: 'Bring the deaf and dumb to me.'" As I stood up to speak that night, I thought, "God, I can't ask people to bring the deaf and dumb to me!" But God spoke to me and said, "Trevor, you didn't hear Me right this afternoon. I did not mean bring them to you – I meant bring them to Me." So at the crusade I invited any deaf and dumb people who wanted to meet the Healer to come onto the platform. About a dozen people came and one by one they began to speak. One little boy, deaf and dumb from birth, was carried up by his father. Then he turned to his father and in English, as clear as you could want to hear, said, "I love you, Daddy." The place erupted.

I believe that as I saw the angel of healing, I moved into alignment with God's throne and that all I had to do was what God wanted to do. As you align yourself with God's will, the angelic might of heaven comes to hold back everything that the demonic may seek to do, and to release what God wants to do. After that many people were healed of kidney diseases, kidney stones and gallstones. I asked the people what they thought God did with those stones! I told them I thought that He threw them at the devil! As you read this, may God hold back everything that is against you, that you may be aligned with God's will once again.

Whatever aid we may receive from angels or ministering spirits it is always designed to bring us into a greater awareness of the anointing we experience with the Holy Spirit.

Chapter 7
Mantles of Anointing

Your mantle

In ancient biblical times a "mantle" was an outer cloak that a person would wear on top of their clothing. It was worn essentially for extra warmth, but could also serve as a symbol of a person's authority. The Hebrew word add-deh-reth (used to describe the mantle of Elijah) means "outer garment", but the root of this word means "power". Because of this connotation, in various places in Scripture the word translated "mantle" expresses the concept of authority and this is the sense in which I use the word in this chapter. But we are speaking about an authority that encompasses the two types of power referred to in the Bible, dunamis (meaning "energy, power, might, force or ability") and exousia (meaning "the authority or right to act, ability, privilege, capacity, delegated authority"). Since all Christians have been anointed and empowered by the Holy Spirit, and should exercise spiritual authority, we need to ask what special manifestations of dunamis and exousia a person who has received a mantle of authority from God might expect to find in their lives. We can suggest several answers to that question.

First, a person who has received a mantle has an anointing that he or she can step into repeatedly. For example, either during a crusade overseas or whilst in our home church, God allows me to operate in a ministry of healing. It's always there, carried as a mantle of healing. This is in contrast with an anointing that is short-term, possibly given for a particular occasion or to meet one particular need.

Second, a person with a mantle of anointing is likely to be extensively used in imparting that anointing to others. This is important because God does not want the anointing to die with us; He wants our anointing to be imparted to equip and further the ministry of the Kingdom.

Finally, following on from these, people who have received a mantle can be expected to be used to spread the anointing geographically, to serve the Lord of all the earth, as seen by Zechariah.

Serving the Lord of all the earth

"Then the angel who talked with me returned and woke me up, like someone awakened from sleep. He asked me, 'What do you see?' I answered, 'I see a solid gold lampstand with a bowl at the top and seven lamps on it, with seven channels to the lamps. Also there are two olive trees by it, one on the right of the bowl

and the other on its left.' I asked the angel who talked with me, 'What are these, my lord?' He answered, 'Do you not know what these are?' 'No, my lord,' I replied. So he said to me, 'This is the word of the Lord to Zerubbabel[5]: "Not by might nor by power, but by my Spirit," says the Lord Almighty. "What are you, mighty mountain? Before Zerubbabel you will become level ground. Then he will bring out the capstone to shouts of 'God bless it! God bless it!'"' Then the word of the Lord came to me: 'The hands of Zerubbabel have laid the foundation of this temple; his hands will also complete it. Then you will know that the Lord Almighty has sent me to you. Who dares despise the day of small things, since the seven eyes of the Lord that range throughout the earth will rejoice when they see the chosen capstone in the hand of Zerubbabel?' Then I asked the angel, 'What are these two olive trees on the right and the left of the lampstand?'
Again I asked him, 'What are these two olive branches beside the two gold pipes that pour out golden oil?' He replied, 'Do you not know what these are?' 'No, my lord,' I said. So he said, 'These are the two who are anointed to serve the Lord of all the earth.'"
(Zechariah 4:1-14)

At the time of Zechariah's vision, Zerubbabel, governor of Judah, and Joshua, the High Priest, had played a leading part in restoring the altar, but were now finding it difficult to persuade the people to carry on with the work of rebuilding the temple. The word given by the angel to Zechariah came as a great encouragement to Zerubbabel, under whose hands the work was indeed completed.

As Zechariah questioned the angel about the fuller meaning

of the vision, he was told that the two olive trees represented Zerubbabel and Joshua, two who were anointed to serve the Lord, a twin source of oil for God's lamp in Jerusalem.

We have here a view of the ministry of Jesus, the pouring out of God's anointed, the Messiah. Today His anointing flows to the Church and the anointed Church is to serve the Lord of all the earth. Jesus spoke prophetically about this relationship with the Church in the prayer recounted in John 17:22-3:

"I have given them the glory that You gave Me, that they may be one as We are one: 'I in them and you in Me.'"

A vision of the olive grove

When Jesus had finished praying, He and His disciples went to the olive grove[6] where they often met (John 18:1-2). I believe that there is a spiritual "olive grove" where Jesus' disciples can meet with Him today.

In October 2001, during a missions trip in Shilong, India, I was taking time preparing, listening to music, soaking and meditating on the Word. I asked God to take me to a deeper place. Suddenly, it was as though He was standing there saying, "I am going to take you down into the olive grove, because the olive grove is the place I love to retire to with My disciples." A vision opened up and I was part of it. A pathway led down into an olive grove. The pathway was covered with the blossoms of the olive trees. The blossoms were so thick that they absorbed the sound of my footsteps; they muffled all sound; it was a place of wonderful solitude.

As I looked down further into the olive grove, I saw that these were olive trees that carried anointing. The first olive tree I saw had men and women standing around it. The first person I saw was Smith Wigglesworth. I looked again and there was Katherine Kuhlman and many others. I looked again and saw the disciples. They were all standing under the olive tree with oil pouring onto them.

Then I saw another olive tree. Around it stood the people with prophetic voices. I looked and began to see figures of prophetic men and women of God. Oil began to run down on them until they were covered with oil. I looked down again and there were other trees with objects hanging from the branches. The branches of the prophetic tree were bearing trumpets. There was a tree of anointing for teaching – not just expounding the Word, but teaching out of revelation and anointing. One of the figures I saw was Derek Prince, a foremost teacher of the Word who moved in revelation.

Jesus wants us to come to the place where we sit under the olive tree, resting in His presence. It takes time for enough oil to drip on us to cover us, time to develop that relationship out of which we receive a mantle of anointing.

At times we may receive an impartation, when people lay hands on us and we receive empowerment for what God wants to do in and through us at a specific moment in time. This can be a powerful experience and result in us operating in a greater level of anointing. We need to be relationally aligned with anointed men and women of God, so that we become aligned with the anointing they carry. But we are not looking only for a brief impartation, but a lasting relationship. As such relationships grow and are strengthened, so too the corporate anointing of those believers will strengthen and increase. I believe this is one of the key principles the Church needs to practice as we move forward together.

Intimacy with Jesus

Most of us will have been invited to attend a wedding ceremony and reception at some point, but only the bridal couple get to spend the night together in the bridal chamber. The time will come when all of us are invited to the wedding supper of the Lamb – a collective spiritual union of the Church with Christ, the culmination of the history of the cosmos. At present, "The creation waits in eager expectation for the sons of God to be revealed" (Romans 8:19). In the meantime, unlike an earthly wedding, every one of us is invited to enjoy the relationship of intimacy which Jesus offers. He longs to take each of us into that place where there is complete oneness with Him.

God wants to take us into a place, a tent of meeting, where He woos our heart and every fibre of our being is touched by His presence. In that place we are totally undone, so that we cannot stand; we become like Moses who, "...could not enter the Tent of Meeting because the cloud had settled upon it, and the glory of the Lord filled the tabernacle" (Exodus 40:35) or like the priests who "...could not enter the temple of the Lord because the glory of the Lord filled it" (2 Chronicles 7:2).

These were moments of the special favour of God, which occurred after the completion of the tabernacle and temple, built according to the pattern shown to Moses. But in my vision of the heavenly olive grove, I heard Jesus say, "Trevor, we are going to return to this place often, because I have more for you." When God's glory filled the temple, Israel responded with thanksgiving and worship. This will, I believe, be our response as we meet Jesus in the heavenly olive grove.

Time in His presence

As I mentioned, some of the people I saw in my vision were sitting under the olive tree so long that they were covered or "mantled" with oil. We need to spend time resting in the Lord's presence, receiving from Him. But as we consider the life of the olive tree, we see that this resting is only part of the story. The olive tree takes seven years before it produces any olives. One tree can produce up to a million blossoms, but only a small portion of the blossoms produce olives. In my vision I saw the ground covered with blossoms. The tree reaches its prime between ten and fifteen years, but it has the ability to continue to produce for about six hundred years.

This teaches me that some time may elapse before the oil begins to flow, both for the olive tree and for me. And this is a time when I need to press in with prayer and fasting, seeking God's face and His anointing. We must press in forcibly. Matthew 11:12 (NKJV) states, "The Kingdom of heaven suffers violence, and the violent take it by force." Some of us give up too quickly. An olive tree can seem to be dead in the ground, but digging around in the top soil causes it to burst into bloom again. It then continues to produce year after year.

The room of mantles

In 1997, while on an extended fast, forcibly pressing in for the things God had put in my heart, I awoke at 4 o'clock one morning. I had a vision in which I received a purple cloak. God told me, "It contains the anointing for ruling; My authority and power." I was then carried in the Spirit into a room where mantles were being made.

There I saw angels making mantles which were being given to people. The mantles covered them from head to foot. In some of the mantles were pockets. When I asked what the pockets were for, the angels said, "They contain the righteous acts that have been prepared beforehand for the saints to do." The people began to take out the righteous acts, to see what had been prepared beforehand for them to do. I concluded that if they have been prepared beforehand, then these things must be somewhere! They are not floating around, they are in the mantles of anointing. In other words, there is a simple process to effectiveness in our Christian lives: we spend time dwelling in the presence of God, waiting on Him – figuratively, under His olive tree – until we are immersed in the oil of His Holy Spirit's anointing. Then we find that we are equipped and able to carry out those good works that God has prepared beforehand for us to do.

In my vision God told me that there was a door at the end of the room, a door I had not noticed before. I went through the door into another room which was filled with flashing light. There were more mantles in there and when I asked, "What are these?" He said, "These are the mantles for ministers." In that room was the five-fold gifting. These mantles looked exactly the same as the others, but as they were held up, it was as if the lightning bolts of God penetrated and permeated these mantles which were then given to individuals.

As I went into the room, God said, "There is a mantle here for you as a minister" and the angels said, "Let us put it on you." As they put it on, it was as if the glowing light of God shone all around me. I could see it. Wearing the mantle, I was asked if I wanted to walk out of the door, as that was when the mantle would come into its function. As I walked towards the door I heard the Spirit of the Lord say to me, "You have to take it off before you can walk through that door." "Why, Lord?" I asked. "So that you can turn it inside out," came the reply. As I did so, I saw that the inside was earthen brown; there was nothing spectacular about it. As I put it on, inside out, the Spirit of the Lord said, "Now, don't you realise?" "Realise what Lord?" I asked. "You will carry the anointing closer to you this way, than you ever would with people seeing it."

My prayer for you is that as you remind yourself of the mantles of anointing that have been imparted and prophesied to you, as you begin to ask God to reveal this to you, that you will experience a deeper level of anointing that impacts all areas of your life and that you will truly realise the fullness of the anointing that God has for you.

Chapter 8
Mantles and
Relationships

Saints who have gone before

Continuing our discussion about mantles, in this chapter I want us to consider the connection between mantles and our relationships with other people. We start by taking a brief look at the importance of our relationships with the saints who have gone before and then consider how we might receive a mantle from those who are currently moving in the anointing today.

We may receive a mantle of anointing when someone prays and imparts something to us, perhaps at a conference, as a one-off experience. We can definitely receive from God in this way. But God is a God of relationship and something altogether more powerful can be produced if we work to develop an ongoing relationship with someone who operates under that same mantle. The relationship that was formed between Elisha and

Elijah is the best scriptural example of this.

Over the past decade we have seen the death of several people who themselves had mantles of anointing and had links with previous moves of God. I think of Bill Bright who had direct links with the Azusa Street revival and was also connected to Leonard Ravenhill, a British evangelist who had a lifelong burden to pray for revival. This burden was taken up by Bill who, during his lifetime, mobilised over three million people to pray for worldwide revival. Kenneth Hagin, who also died in recent years, had direct links with the latter rain and Word of Faith movement. Ern Baxter, an anointed Bible teacher, had links to William Branham who, more than anyone else in the last century, operated in an incredible level of the word of knowledge and healing miracles.[7]

In the United Kingdom, there was Bryn Jones who led Harvestime, a new church movement in the UK in the 1970s and 80s When he was a young man, he knew people who had lived through the Welsh revival and later had links with healing evangelists such as George Jeffreys. In the 1960s, when the basement of Kensington Temple was being cleared (and for which there is photographic evidence), the workers found wheelchairs in which people had come to George Jeffreys' campaigns. They were abandoned as the cripples were healed. In Birmingham there are medical records of terminally ill patients which read, "Taken to George Jeffreys' meeting and discharged."

Parents store up an inheritance

The Scriptures tell us that it is not children who store up an inheritance, but their parents who store it up for their children. I believe that the death of these saints I have mentioned, as well as others you will know about, will lead to an unprecedented release of the Spirit – a release that could result in an extension of God's Kingdom on the earth, as Israel's Kingdom was extended when David was succeeded as King by his son Solomon.

We must take care that we do nothing that would cause the Kingdom to splinter, as happened after Solomon's death. There must be no competition between ministries or criticism of other ministries. If our ministry is unjustly criticised, as it sometimes can be if we are moving in the power of God, we must refuse to take offence.

The mantle passes from Moses to Joshua

When Moses died, God chose Joshua as his successor. The mantle carried by Moses passed to Joshua. The time had come for Israel to take possession of the land promised by God to Abraham. A prime requirement was for a leader who had been tested in battle and the first time we meet Joshua is when he is waging war against the Amalekites. Joshua overcame the Amelekites, but in doing so he learned that military prowess and wisdom may not be sufficient. Moses sat on a hill overlooking the battle and only when he continued to hold up his hands did Joshua prevail. The battle was won because, "hands were lifted up to the throne of the Lord" (Exodus 17:12-13, 15).

In Exodus chapter 32 we read that when Moses was coming down the mountain carrying the tablets of the Testimony, he and Joshua heard the shouts of the people. Joshua thought that this meant that a battle was being waged, but Moses knew that it was a sound of singing, of celebration. Joshua had to learn to discern what was going on.

He also had to learn what God was doing. In Numbers chapter 11 God told Moses to bring seventy of the elders to the Tent of Meeting, where "I will take of the Spirit that is on you and put the Spirit on them" (Numbers 11:17). In this way Moses would be able to share the burden of leadership. Although two of the elders chosen by Moses, Elded and Medad, remained in the camp, God still put His Spirit on them and they prophesied in the camp. Joshua, completely misreading the situation, told Moses to stop them.

But Moses told him that, on the contrary, "I wish that all the Lord's people were prophets and that the Lord would put his Spirit on them" (Numbers 11:29).

If Moses and Joshua had not been in relationship, how do you think Joshua would have felt at times like these? "I thought that I understood – that I was beginning to move in discernment – and he tells me that I totally missed the point." Joshua had to learn to grow in such situations so that he would be worthy to receive the mantle of Moses.

Elijah and Elisha

In 1 Kings chapter 19 we read how, at a time when Elijah was feeling that his life had been wasted, God told him to, "anoint Elisha ... to succeed you as prophet" (1 Kings 19:16). When Elijah found Elisha he threw his mantle around him. This was the sign that Elisha would inherit the authority in which Elijah moved. However, Elijah had been given other commissions from God and he needed to retain his mantle until these had been fulfilled. The only thing we read about Elisha in the following years was that he gave up farming and served Elijah.

As Elisha served Elijah, he would have heard him deliver prophetic words and seen him perform miracles. This experience surely increased his desperation to receive Elijah's mantle and even a double portion. So as Elijah's death drew near, Elisha would not let him out of his sight.

Their final journey – receiving a double portion!

Elijah and Elisha travelled to Gilgal – significant because this was the place where, when Israel entered the promised land, Joshua had circumcised all the men who were born in the desert during the journey from Egypt. It became a place of consecration and covenant. Before he was circumcised, Abraham tried to accomplish God's will in his own strength and fathered Ishmael. After he was circumcised he fathered Isaac, the child of promise. In circumcision the strength of the flesh is cut. When our hearts are circumcised the power of the Spirit flows.

From Gilgal to Bethel

From Gilgal[8], Elijah was then sent by the Lord to Bethel[9], the House of God, and he tried to dissuade Elisha from following. But Elisha was determined to accompany him. This is the only time we hear of Elisha being "disobedient". Elisha refused the rejection that Elijah tried to place upon him. It seems that the other prophets might also have tried to dissuade Elisha from following, asking whether he realised that the Lord was about to take Elijah. But Elisha refused to be diverted.

From Bethel to Jericho

Elijah tried to persuade Elisha to stay in Bethel while he went on to Jericho, but again his tactic was to no avail. One of the meanings of Jericho is "place of fragrance". But we also know that Jericho was a place where no one went in and no one came out. To release the fragrance, God flattened the place and the stones remained as a sign of God's power.

From Jericho to the Jordan

Finally Elijah headed for the Jordan[10], and he tested Elisha's commitment, loyalty and determination for one last time. The Jordan speaks of God's faithfulness. When Israel had crossed the Jordan, they picked up stones to build a memorial to God's faithfulness in fulfilling His promises. All of God's promises are yes and amen in Christ and the cross is our reminder of His eternal covenant of promise.

Elijah struck the Jordan with his mantle and the waters parted. The Jordan was a place of separation. Elisha had been separated from Elijah – but he had received his mantle!

The prophets wanted to go and look for Elijah and finally Elisha allowed them to go, but he knew that their search would be fruitless. When we are parted from fleshly ambition and begin to flow in the anointing, we do not want to go back to where we were.

Learning and receiving

In learning from the experience of Joshua and Elisha, it seems that as they observed what was said and done by Moses and Elijah, they were being prepared to receive their mantles. I believe that the same principle applies today. From our relationships with others who are moving in the power of the Spirit, we too can learn and be prepared. We can then receive an anointing and even a mantle.

You can receive an inheritance today, during the lifetime of your spiritual fathers. As I reflect on my own life I find that I can distinguish four types of relationships that I have had with people whom I consider to be spiritual fathers.

Arthur Neil: a deliverance mantle

Arthur Neil was one of the first people to move in deliverance in Britain in the 1970s, and was a lecturer at the college I attended. Sharon and I spent three years with Arthur during our time at the Bible College of Wales in Swansea, and he would invite us over, sharing with us about his supernatural experiences.

He told us that one day he went to his church office unusually early one morning. He didn't really understand why he had decided to do this, as he tended to arrive at the church around the same time everyday, but as he walked into the church He heard God say to him, "There is resurrection life here." As Arthur sat at his desk he heard someone entering the church and then footsteps coming down the corridor towards his office. Thinking it strange that anyone should come to the church at that early hour, he got up and immediately opened his study door. Outside stood a woman who looked shocked to see Arthur. She saw Arthur, froze, dropped a bag on the floor and then ran out of the building.

Arthur had been involved in bringing the witch Doreen Irving out of the occult. This woman who had entered the church was linked with Doreen's occult past. Not understanding what had happened, Arthur picked up the bag and opened it. In it was a carving knife and a suicide note in handwriting identical to Arthur's own, with his signature. The woman had planned to hide in Arthur's study and murder him when he arrived. Such a sinister plot had been intercepted and uncovered because Arthur obeyed God and went to church earlier than normal, therefore surprising his assailant and preventing the event from taking place. He told us, "I do not know why I got there at that time in the morning. Only God knows. If I had been ten minutes later, that person could have been hiding in my office when I walked in and my life would have ended. That day I knew that God had taken me into a new place."

Randy Clark: an apostolic mantle

My relationship with Randy Clark has been of a different nature. It has been more sporadic than with Arthur Neil, but equally significant. The first time I heard Randy speak was at the 1994 Catch the Fire Conference in Toronto. He told us how he had become disillusioned with his life as a pastor and had a great hunger for more of God. I see him now as an apostolic figure in this move of the Spirit. On one of my many subsequent visits to

Toronto, I met Randy and he invited me to join him for coffee. For half an hour I absorbed everything he shared with me.

On an earlier occasion, as Randy prayed for people at the end of a meeting, I was his catcher for about two and a half hours. I had told him, "I will catch for you all night. If anyone is not receiving, it can come over into me." At the end of the night, not knowing what Sharon and I were about to do, as Randy prayed for me he said, "God is going to take you to the nation of India and you are going to receive revelation there. You are going to be caught up into a new dimension with God there. There is a commissioning angel who carries healing and an anointing to preach the Gospel with signs and wonders. You are going to be taken up, sucked up in this whirlwind." At the time I did not see anything. I did not receive a great, glorious revelation of the heavenly domain. But I knew that I was in an entirely new place!

Some years later, again in Toronto, when Randy called leaders to the front, about a thousand people went forward, including Sharon and myself. Randy walked up and down, praying quietly in the Spirit. Suddenly he stopped and said, "Trevor, there is an anointing of Wigglesworth coming on you for healing. It is going to be a mantle of anointing coming upon you."

The mantle of Smith Wigglesworth – apostle of faith

The week before English evangelist Smith Wigglesworth[11] died, David Du Plessis, one of the main founders of the Charismatic movement asked him, "Mr Wigglesworth, who are you going to give your mantle to when you die?" He replied, "I am not done with it myself yet." Wigglesworth died. He did not leave his mantle to anyone. But I believe that a mantle of anointing was left for the Church. God's desire was to equip not just one, but many saints for the work of preaching the Gospel with signs and wonders. On one occasion I found myself ministering in the church where Wigglesworth himself had been based. As God's presence overwhelmed me, I found myself rolling around on the carpet. Recalling Randy's words, I asked God to impart as much of Wigglesworth's anointing to me as I could handle.

I literally "felt" an anointing of healing coming upon my life. After that event, healings in ministry times began to increase and I experienced the first creative miracle I'd ever seen while in India, praying for a baby who grew two new eyes! As I recall the experience, I am aware that the time this happened was March 12, 1997, a year significant for being exactly fifty years after Wigglesworth's death. This was a year of jubilee in biblical terms – a year when everything is restored back to the family line. I believe God was restoring back to the Church the healing mantle that Wigglesworth kept as an individual, but which needed to be released to the whole Church.

Bill Johnson: a culture of revival

I believe that Bill Johnson carries a mantle of revival, but I have used the word culture because what Bill carries permeates his entire church in Redding, California, and is leaking out through ordinary people's lives. Bill tells how one day, someone phoned to ask if he could join the evangelistic team when it went into the mall on the following Saturday. Bill told him that they didn't have an evangelistic team, but the caller replied, "Oh yes you have. They have been in the mall today. I saw them. They have been witnessing and people in the mall are being healed and having prophetic words spoken over their lives." Bill repeated, "We haven't got an evangelistic team." Then the penny dropped. "Oh, you mean the people in our church who go shopping?"

A principle for all

I am aware that I am very privileged to be able to spend time with so many anointed people, and that I have had opportunities that may not be open to everyone. But I believe that these opportunities have arisen partly because of my determination to press in and take hold of all God has for me. I also believe that everyone, to a greater or lesser extent, can adopt the principle of seeking out and spending as much time as possible in the presence of those who carry mantles of anointing.

Chapter 9
The Kingdom
of Heaven

The kingdom and our inheritance from Adam

We are living in amazing days. God is pouring out His Spirit on a scale that has not been seen within living memory. People speak of fresh moves of God, of new wine, revivals and outpourings and rightly so! These new moves serve an ancient purpose, first revealed to Adam.

God created man to be fruitful, to increase, to have dominion over and subdue the earth. Adam's commission was to extend, through his life, the rule and reign of God on earth. When God breathed life into Adam he became a man of two worlds[12], a man of the dust and a man of the Spirit, unlike any other created being.

Adam's first experience of the angelic was the seraphim who wielded a flaming sword to deny him access to the tree of life after the fall. We now have a sword, the sword of the Spirit, the Word of God. This sword is more powerful than any sword made by man. "It penetrates even to dividing soul and spirit, joints and marrow; it judges the thoughts and attitudes of the heart" (Hebrews 4:12). This is not a sword that prevents us from entering into life, but one which allows us to experience the fullness of the life of God on earth. We too are people of dust and the Spirit. As God reigns in our hearts and our lives His Kingdom is extended and His purpose is restored.

The fundamental basis of this restoration is the cross. Jesus' death was an event to which everything looked forward, even from the time of God's rebuke of Satan in Eden. Since then man can say, "We do not know when the end will come, but the breakthrough of the end hangs over us as an ever present cloud of glorious promise."[13] Jesus was completely aware of the present and coming glory.

John the Baptist

John the Baptist saw a cloud of promise when he recognised Jesus as the Lamb of God. But when he was imprisoned he began to have doubts. John sent his disciples to ask Jesus, "Are you the One who was to come, or should we expect someone else?" (Matthew 11:3). John was a forerunner who prepared the way for the message and the messenger. While in his mother's womb he leapt for joy when Mary greeted his mother, Elizabeth. He truly was a man of the Spirit and of dust.

But, it seems, he began to doubt the Spirit's witness. John was probably expecting the Messiah to be like other conquering kings, not one who would leave His servants to languish in prison.

Jesus told John's disciples to take back a report of the many signs that God's Kingdom had broken through:

"The blind receive sight, the lame walk, those who have leprosy are cured, the deaf hear, the dead are raised, and the good news is preached to the poor." (Matthew 11:5)

We too, like John, need to hear reassuring accounts of what Jesus is doing. Like John, we can all experience times when we do not see God act as we would like and begin to ask why He does not seem to be moving where we are. Jesus then began to speak to the crowd about John. They had rightly seen him as a prophet, but he was more than a prophet, verse 10 says, "This is the one about whom it is written: 'I will send My messenger ahead of You, who will prepare Your way before You.'"

Prophecy and breakthrough

Jesus continued to speak to the crowd:

"From the days of John the Baptist until now, the Kingdom of Heaven has been forcefully advancing, and forceful men lay hold of it: For all the Prophets and the Law prophesied until John. And if you are willing to accept it, he is the Elijah who was to come." (Matthew 11:12-13)

John's prophetic word had heralded the breakthrough of God's Kingdom. He spoke words of destiny concerning Jesus, the Lamb of God, the One on whom the Spirit remained and who would baptise with the Holy Spirit and fire.

A breakthrough of God's Kingdom or a new stage in a person's destiny is often prefaced by a prophetic word, spoken by men or by angels. In very different ways, Samuel and Nathan spoke words that released David into his destiny, who served the purpose of God in his generation.

When a prophetic word is given, a response should follow. When Nathan spoke to David, his response was to repent and cry out to God for mercy. Another response – after David was anointed by Samuel – was for David to challenge and kill Goliath. Our own responses to God have been many and varied – to move house, pray, bid for properties, and start nightly meetings, to name but a few.

All of these involved considerable sacrifice and cost. I believe that unless we respond, in whatever way is appropriate, the prophecy will lie fallow; it will not be activated. It is time for you to remind yourself of the prophetic words spoken over your life. Do not allow them to lie dormant any longer. Begin to pray into them, contend for them and see your life transformed as you experience breakthrough.

Prophetic words that transformed my life

My own life and ministry have been greatly impacted as I have responded to prophetic words given to me. In 2008, as we celebrated the tenth anniversary of Revival Fires, I reflected on three words that have been especially significant. After receiving the first word from British revivalist Ken Gott, a Pentecostal

Pastor from the North East of England, we immediately put our house up for sale and made plans to move from Telford to Dudley. There we started a church with eight people (in Scripture eight is symbolic of new beginnings), meeting in a hotel lounge. Later, we bought the Grace Centre as our church base.

The second word was given by Bobby Conner, a good friend and an outstanding seer prophet from Moravian Falls, at one of our conferences in Dudley. He said that our church would become an Apostolic Resource Centre which would be used to equip and send out many people. I grasped hold of this word and, after several years of contending for it in prayer, we bought a large furniture factory and showroom which is now the Apostolic Resource Centre. The ARC is the location for our conferences, for the Equipped for Supernatural Living, Revival Fires' twelve month School of Ministry, for our walk-in Healing Clinic and for our local church meetings and events.

The third and most recent major word was given to me by Todd Bentley when he prayed for me in Lakeland in 2008. He said that I was to take what was happening in Lakeland back to Dudley, the greater Birmingham area, and the United Kingdom, and he prophetically gave me a hot coal.

We responded by holding nightly meetings. The first meeting was held at very short notice and with very little publicity – we made a brief video and posted it to our website!

The meeting was due to start at 7.30pm, but the queue outside the church began to form at 3 o'clock in the afternoon, and by the start of the meeting 1,000 people had turned up from many parts of the United Kingdom.

The Kingdom: visible and audible

When the Kingdom broke in at Jesus' baptism there was a visible manifestation: the Spirit descended on Him like a dove. There was an audible voice from heaven that proclaimed, "You are My Son, whom I love; with You I am well pleased" (Luke 3:22). This prefigured Jesus' ministry. He both announced the good news of the Kingdom and demonstrated it by healing and delivering people and by raising the dead.

Writing in 1 Corinthians 2:2-5, Paul said,

"I resolved to know nothing while I was with you except Christ Jesus and him crucified; I came to you in weakness and fear, and with much trembling. My message and my preaching were not with wise and persuasive words, but with a demonstration of the Spirit's power, so that your faith might not rest on men's wisdom, but on God's power."

We need to proclaim that Jesus went about both preaching and demonstrating the Kingdom. This proclamation raises peoples' expectancy that they will see God's rule and reign manifest.

The resurrection

The cross is the fundamental basis of the restoration of God's Kingdom on earth. At the cross, God's wrath was poured out on man's sin as Jesus drank the cup of wrath. God's judgement, that the wages of sin is death, was carried out. When Jesus rose from the dead, the penalty for sin having been paid, He demonstrated that sin's power had finally been broken. It no longer had power over Him or over us. And "If we have been united with Him like this in His death, we will certainly also be united with Him in His resurrection" (Romans 6:5). When we accept the Lord Jesus Christ as our Saviour, we no longer fear judgement to come because our sin has already been judged. For us, Calvary was "the day of vengeance of our God" (Isaiah 61:2).

But for those who are outside of the Lord Jesus Christ, the day of God's vengeance lies ahead. When Jesus read from the scroll of Isaiah 61 in the synagogue, the Scripture that was to be fulfilled included the proclamation of the year of the Lord's favour. It did not extend to the day of the vengeance of God, because that was to be fulfilled later. Jesus would also have been familiar with an earlier, more comprehensive, prophecy, contained in chapter 35 of Isaiah. We will continue these thoughts in the final chapter.

Chapter 10
Keys of the Kingdom

The keys of the Kingdom

In the book of Revelation we see the centrality of the Lord Jesus emphasised in the process of man's restoration. To the church at Philadelphia, Jesus speaks of Himself as One, "who is holy and true, who holds the key of David" (Revelation 3:7). This speaks of Jesus' fulfilment of a further prophecy of Isaiah that says,

"I will place on his shoulder the key to the house of David; what he opens no-one can shut, and what he shuts no-one can open. I will drive him like a peg into a firm place; he will be a seat of honour for the house of his father. All the glory of his family will hang on him; its offspring and offshoots – all its lesser vessels, from the bowls to all the jars." (Isaiah 22:22-24)

A key represents ownership. We have been sealed with the Holy Spirit as a deposit, guaranteeing our full inheritance (2 Corinthians 1:21-22 and see also Ephesians 1:11, Colossians 1:12 and 1 Peter 1:3-5). Jesus has set His seal of ownership upon us. A key means that you are the rightful owner of that which the key has access to. We have the anointing that gives us access to our inheritance.

The key of David – the key of kingship, authority, government – is placed on the shoulder of Jesus, the increase of whose government will never end. Jesus uses the key of authority to open some doors but to close others. Paul was prevented by the Holy Spirit from preaching the word in Asia and from entering Bithynia, but then he was called to Macedonia and later to Ephesus, "because a great door for effective work has opened to me" (1 Corinthians 16:8-9). Jesus opens the doors to the "good works which God prepared in advance for us to do" (Ephesians 2:10).

Jesus told the church in Philadelphia, "I know your deeds. See I have placed before you an open door that no-one can shut. I know that you have little strength, yet you have kept My word and have not denied My name" (Revelation 3:8). There is a spiritual empowerment that comes to those who wait upon the Lord.

An encounter with the key of David

While I was on holiday one summer recently, and in that half asleep, half awake moment, I was woken up into a fresh God-encounter. It was like "the visions that passed through my mind while I lay on my bed" experience that Daniel had. Daniel could perhaps have been in a dream-like state or it could have been that he was just pondering the presence of God. That's what I felt I was doing.

In the encounter, I saw God offering me something and He said to me, "I'm giving you the key of David." I was thinking, "No, God must mean the keys of the Kingdom that are mentioned in Matthew 16:19. However, God said, "No, I'm giving you the key of David." As I looked at His hand, however, I saw that it was empty. There was nothing in it at all. So I asked the Lord, "What is the key of David?" God told me, "The key is the anointing that David carried." The key is for ruling and reigning. It is a symbol of ownership, access, authority and influence.

A new dimension of the anointing

Do you want to move into a new level, a new place of anointing? Do you want a key that will open effective doors of ministry for you? Then, take hold of the key of David. Right now, God is offering you a new dimension of anointing that will be like a key in a door that will open the next realm, the next sphere of your influence of the anointing, of the Kingdom working and operating through you. Do you want that? I want that not just for Dudley, but for the UK and the nations!

Isaiah 22:22

The key of David first appears in Scripture in Isaiah 22:22, the prophecy of Isaiah mentioned earlier in relation to Jesus:

"The key of the house of David I will lay on His shoulder; So he shall open, and no one shall shut; And he shall shut, and no one shall open." (NKJV)

This is a key that's set in a secure place, that opens situations, doors and opportunities and no man can shut them. With this key Jesus closes things and no man can open them. What a powerful key!

An open door

I believe that God is going to open doors in your life as you read this today. You can have closure to sickness, sickness that is like a prison to you. There are also other harmful areas in your lives that God is going to shut. Even ministry can become a prison. Sometimes we can get into a pastoral prison, which rather than opening things for us, restricts us. In that restrictive place, God needs to bring closure. He closes the door and says, "You are not going back there." So often we want the "open door," but sometimes we need God to close doors. This is what the key of David does.

Keys given to Peter

When Peter acknowledged Jesus as the Christ, the Son of the Living God, Jesus said "I will give you the keys of the Kingdom of heaven" (Matthew 16:16, 19).

Peter's authority was seen when he released God's word and a demonstration of the Holy Spirit's power, first into the Jewish

Church and then, at Cornelius' house, into the Gentile world.

I believe that when the risen Jesus said, "All authority in heaven and on earth has been given to me. Therefore go and make disciples of all nations..." (Matthew 28:18-19), He was declaring that His disciples are given the keys to the Kingdom. Under the Lord's guidance we are to preach the Kingdom, heal the sick, cast out demons and raise the dead. We are also to equip others for the work of ministry, so that God's Kingdom might be further extended.

24-7 access

The key gives us ownership and access. When you have the key, you have access any time. You don't have, for example, the key to my car or my house. Those who do have access to those things can have access any time. We don't need to pray to God to "rend the heavens" (Isaiah 64:1) because we already have access to heaven 24-7 through the cross of Jesus – in fact we are already seated in heavenly places. There is an access in the Spirit that opens doors into those heavenly places and they are real geographical realms in the Spirit that we can access with that key.[14]

Authority

Do you know that this key also gives you authority? I have the key to my house, I don't have the key to your house. I have no authority to walk into your house. If I do, I am an intruder, a trespasser. But I can take my key and walk into my house any time I want because I have the authority to do it. So, the key speaks of authority.

The anointing also speaks of authority. I believe God wants to put a new authority upon your life to empower you to do what Jesus has decreed you would do when He commissioned you as one of His disciples – the same commission that He gave to His first disciples: to heal the sick, raise the dead, cleanse the lepers and drive out demons. Why can Jesus tell us to do these things? Because He has authority and He says to us, "I give you authority." That's the key of David! David had tremendous divinely imparted authority. His kingly anointing from God was such that frequently his enemies were moved out of the way so that he could come right into the place where God wanted him to be.

Full inheritance

For the past few years God has been telling me that the Church is about to enter into its full inheritance, the unlimited resources of heaven.

When I was a boy my father showed me two things that he promised to pass on to me: a silver Morgan dollar and a silver pocket watch. About eighteen months ago, when I asked him what had happened to the dollar he told me that he had given it to my brother. I told him that it did not matter and asked him what had happened to the watch. "You will not believe this," he said, "but I gave that to your brother as well." I was obviously disappointed, but I now see that God was preparing to teach me about His redemptive purposes.

This began when, in a conference in 2007, Canadian prophetic revivalist Charlie Robinson gave me a Canadian silver dollar and declared, "There are redemptive purposes for you." Later in the conference, after I had finished speaking on receiving our full inheritance, a man I didn't know came up to me and gave me an 1878 Morgan silver dollar, saying, "I think that this is the Morgan dollar you should have received." I then went on a ministry trip to South Africa and as we were preparing to return, someone gave us a packet containing a present for Sharon and a present for me. When I opened my packet, I found a lovely silver pocket watch and a coin dated 1906. As I looked at the watch I felt that God was saying to me, "I am restoring your full inheritance. I am restoring a move of the Spirit in your life."

Your inheritance recovered

When the Israelites were preparing to embark on the journey that would lead them to their inheritance, the land promised to them by God, they were given articles of silver together with articles of gold and clothing. On that journey God would manifest His presence, His glory, in the cloud by day and by fire at night. As we enter into our inheritance, God's glory will again be revealed. When we pray, when we speak, He will release His power and the sick will be healed, demons cast out and the dead raised.

When John the Baptist testified about Jesus, he declared, "The one whom God has sent speaks the words of God, for God gives the Spirit without limit. The Father loves the Son and has placed everything in His hands." (John 3:34-5)

Shortly before his death, Smith Wigglesworth prophesied a coming together of the Word and the Spirit which would herald a move of God greater than anything ever seen (and he himself had been used to heal many and raise people from the dead!). Jesus said to His disciples, "'Peace be with you! As the Father has sent Me, I am sending you.' And with that He breathed on them and said, 'Receive the Holy Spirit'" (John 20:21-22). We too are sons of God who have been sent. I believe these are promises that we can choose to embrace and that the time is fast approaching when we too will be given the Spirit without limit.

The greater works

The letter to the Hebrews speaks of those, "who have tasted the heavenly gift, who have shared in the Holy Spirit, who have tasted the goodness of the Word of God and the powers of the coming age" (Hebrews 6:4-5). Paul knew the goodness of God's word: "Faith comes by hearing, and hearing by the word of God" (Romans 10:17). He also knew the importance of operating in the power of the Holy Spirit:

"My message and my preaching were not with wise and persuasive words, but with a demonstration of the Spirit's power, so that your faith might not rest on man's wisdom, but on God's power" (1 Corinthians 2:4-5).

I believe that the time is coming when we who have tasted will feast fully at the Lord's table.

The Church is moving into a place where it becomes the fullness of the measure of the stature of Christ – so that we begin to do the things that Jesus did in the same power and authority. And this won't be through one individual, but through a body moving into a dimension of the anointing that releases the power of the age to come do the "greater works" that Jesus declared we would do.

And as the body of Christ, the Church, moves into a greater dimension of that anointing, we will do the same things that Jesus did and the "greater things", and we will carry an incredible degree of authority because He is the Head and we move under the anointing of His Headship.

Impartation from reading this book!

I believe God wants to impart an anointing to you from this book, to have an outpouring similar to what happened in Dudley in 2008. He really does! There is also an anointing here to give you authority, to see the supernatural realms released, to move you into a new place where you take ownership of the anointing that God wants to give you. I want to release what God has given to me by giving it away freely as you read this, giving out what God has given me. In Matthew 10:8 it says, "Freely you have received, freely give."

Throughout this book I have sought to take you on a journey that I've been on in accessing the supernatural realms of heaven. I believe there are three key principles that I have sought to underline, which I conclude with here.

The first principle is to set aside times where you intentionally press into God to receive. This may include prayer and fasting, waiting in His presence and meditating on His Word.

The second principle is to stir up a desire for the miraculous.

The way that I've done this is to read testimonies of those who moved in signs, wonders and miracles. I look at their lives and characters and study the ways in which they were used as a channel through which miracles could flow into the lives of others. I've also taken a pen and marked every miracle that can be found in Scripture and used those Scriptures as a means of meditating and opening myself up to God to do the same things through me.

The third principle is to seek out those who carry the anointing. There have been times in my life when I have seen other men and women flowing in the anointing that I believe God has spoken to me about. So I have sought to go and hear them speak and minister, so that I may connect with what is taking place in the environment where they are flowing with the Holy Spirit. As we spend time in such an environment, I believe we can "pick up" the anointing.

I have found that as I combine these three principles, my spirit is opened to receive much more of God. My desire is that you too would intentionally pursue the presence of God and that as you do, you would consistently move into new levels of anointing.

Now I ask you to put your hand upon your heart, as I want to release an impartation. Father, I ask that you would impart a fresh desire to pursue your presence. I ask that every anointing that you have stored up for our lives would be released, so that we would flow in a new level of the supernatural. Father, you have said that you are a rewarder of those who diligently seek You. I ask now that you would release that spirit of diligence upon our lives in Jesus' name.

May God bless you as you continue to seek His presence.

Endnotes

1. The Hebrew word naba (Strongs#H5012) means to "bubble up," to prophesy, to speak or sing by inspiration of God.

2. The Hebrew word roeh (Strongs#H7204,7203) – means a prophet or seer – one who receives a lot of revelation from God via dreams and visions. See James Goll's book The Seer.

3. The number three was very significant in Peter's life, so he knew that God was trying to get his attention. Jesus told Peter he would deny Him three times (Matthew 26:34), and Jesus said to Peter three times "Simon, son of Jonah, do you love Me?" (John 21:15-17)

4. Dionysius the Areopagite, was the Athenian convert of the apostle Paul mentioned in Acts17:34. He was also the judge of the Areopagus. The Areopagus or Areios Pagos is the "Hill of Ares," northwest of the Acropolis, which in classical times functioned as the high Court of Appeal for criminal and civil cases in Athens. See http://en.wikipedia.org/wiki/Dionysius_the_Areopagite and http://en.wikipedia.org/wiki/Areopagus

5. Zerubbabel (Strong's # H2215,H894) is a combination of two Hebrew words zarab which means "to flow away" and babel which means "confusion" and can refer to Babylon and it's empire. So, Zerubbabel can be translated as "to flow away from confusion" or "coming out of confusion."

6. Jesus often went to the garden of Gethsemane (see Matthew 26:30,36-56' Luke 22:39; John 18:1-2). Gethsemane (Strong's#G1068) means "oil press," so we too need to go to the garden where the olives are being pressed so we can receive the oil.

7. For more on Ern Baxter see www.ernbaxter.com. There's also a youtube video clip of Ern Baxter talking about William Branham (see

youtube.com – "Ern Baxter on William Branham, Word and Spirit"). For more on William Branham see Book 1 of God's Generals: Why Some Succeeded and Why Some Failed, by Roberts Liardon, chapter ten and there is a five book series on the life of William Branham entitled Supernatural: The Life of William Branham by Owen Jorgensen; also, William Branham, A Man Sent From God, by Gordon Lindsay, written in collaboration with William Branham.

8. 2Kings 2:1.Gilgal (Strongs#H1536 and1537) means "wheel." Gilgal can also be seen as place of obedience. It was at Gilgal, in 1 Samuel 10:8, that Saul was told to wait seven days for the prophet Samuel to come make sacrifices. The seven days passed, Samuel still hadn't come and so Saul disobeyed the word of the Lord Samuel gave him and offered the sacrifice. This disobedience was very costly to Saul, as he would lose the Kingdom of Israel (see 1 Samuel 10:8 and 13:8-14)

9. Bethel, (Beth El, Strongs #H1008)) literally means "House of God." This was the place where Jacob in Genesis 28 had his well known open heavens encounter in a dream. It can be seen as a portal of intimacy, a place spiritually speaking where we minister to the Lord and receive revelation from Him, even a place of soaking. Of course, while there are physical geographical places (portals) where it's easier to receive from God and there may be more angelic activity or where God has something special for you there if you make the journey, we as New Testament believers carry Bethel in us! "Do you not know that you are the temple of God and that the Spirit of God dwells in you?" – 1 Corinthians 3:16 (NKJV). And, "Or do you not know that your body is the temple of the Holy Spirit who is in you, whom you have from God, and you are not your own?" – 1 Corinthians 6:19 (NKJV)

10. Jordan (Strongs# H3383, 3381) means "to descend, going down." When Jesus went to the cross, it looked like the lowest point in His

ministry, such humiliation to be stripped naked, brutally flogged, jeered, mocked and crucified with two thieves. And yet this going down, was actually the greatest point in His earthly ministry! He took all of mankind's punishment for sin (drank the cup of wrath) and in so doing redeemed mankind and established the New Covenant. So, the Jordan can represent the cross.

11. Smith Wigglesworth (1859-1947) was one of the foremost evangelists in England who operated in miracles, signs and wonders and had incredible revelation about faith, see Book 1 of God's Generals: Why Some Succeeded and Why Some Failed, by Roberts Liardon, chapter seven and www.smithwigglesworth.com and http://en.wikipedia.org/wiki/Smith_Wigglesworth. David DuPlessis (1905-1987) was a South African born Pentecostal minister and one of the main founders of the Charismatic movement, see http://en.wikipedia.org/wiki/David_du_Plessis.

12. Jesus, while on earth, also lived in two worlds at the same time – earth and heaven. In Jn3:13, Jesus, while on earth, speaks this to Nicodemus "No one has ascended to heaven but He who came down from heaven, that is the Son of Man who is in heaven [NKJV]."

13. I believe that Derek Morphew, Dean of the Vineyard International School of Theology, first used these words.

14. Heaven, the third heaven (2Cor12:2), is more than the throne room or throne zone of Revelation 4. There are heavenly courts (see Zechariah 3:7), the many rooms of the Father's house (see John 14:2). There is also the house of wine (See SofS2:4-the "banqueting table" literally means "house of wine."

About the Author

TREVOR & SHARON BAKER passionately pursue a life of signs, wonders and miracles. From the outset of founding Revival Fires in 1998, they have seen the power of God increase as they have believed wholeheartedly in the New Testament Church as the standard for today. Trevor and Sharon regularly host conferences at the ARC in Dudley, inviting people into powerful worship and equipping believers to carry supernatural power in their everyday lives. Based in the heart of England, Trevor ministers both as pastor to a growing local church and to the wider body of Christ. He travels internationally as a conference speaker, leads mission trips and mass crusades.